About Island Press

Since 1984, the nonprofit organization Island Press has been stimulating, shaping, and communicating ideas that are essential for solving environmental problems worldwide. With more than 1,000 titles in print and some 30 new releases each year, we are the nation's leading publisher on environmental issues. We identify innovative thinkers and emerging trends in the environmental field. We work with world-renowned experts and authors to develop cross-disciplinary solutions to environmental challenges.

Island Press designs and executes educational campaigns, in conjunction with our authors, to communicate their critical messages in print, in person, and online using the latest technologies, innovative programs, and the media. Our goal is to reach targeted audiences—scientists, policy makers, environmental advocates, urban planners, the media, and concerned citizens—with information that can be used to create the framework for long-term ecological health and human well-being.

Island Press gratefully acknowledges major support from The Bobolink Foundation, Caldera Foundation, The Curtis and Edith Munson Foundation, The Forrest C. and Frances H. Lattner Foundation, The JPB Foundation, The Kresge Foundation, The Summit Charitable Foundation, Inc., and many other generous organizations and individuals.

The opinions expressed in this book are those of the author(s) and do not necessarily reflect the views of our supporters.

BUILDING THE CYCLING CITY

BUILDING THE CYCLING CITY

*The Dutch Blueprint
for Urban Vitality*

MELISSA BRUNTLETT AND

CHRIS BRUNTLETT

◐ **ISLAND**PRESS Washington | Covelo | London

Island Press is a trademark of The Center for Resource Economics.

Library of Congress Control Number: 2018934803

All Island Press books are printed on environmentally responsible materials.

Manufactured in the United States of America
10 9 8 7 6 5 4 3

Keywords: Amsterdam, Atlanta, Austin, *bakfiets*, bicycle, bicycle lane, bicycle parking, bicycle superhighway, Boston, cargo bicycle, Eindhoven, Groningen, Green Lane Project, New York City, Philadelphia, Portland, Rotterdam, safety bicycle, San Francisco, Seattle, transit, urban design, urban planning, Utrecht, Vancouver, Vision Zero

TO CORALIE AND ETIENNE

---

the best adventurers any
parents could ask for.

You are our constant inspiration,
and the reason we keep riding
along on this crazy journey!

CONTENTS

PREFACE

In the summer of 2010, our family of four made a decision that would transform our lives for the better, although not in ways that we ever could have anticipated. After moving just blocks from Commercial-Broadway Station on Vancouver's east side and soon finding our car collecting dust in the parking garage, we decided to ditch it and make all of our trips by foot, bicycle, public transit, and rental car (in the rare instances when we needed to take a road trip).

The decision was solely practical, and not ideological. Living in a compact, walkable neighborhood afforded us the luxury of having everything within a 20-minute walk or 10-minute train ride, which we quickly discovered could be replaced with short bike ride. Best of all, this resulted in an extra $800 in our pockets each month, an incentive enabled by the variety of mobility options offered by our city. This includes car-share, access to which ultimately convinced us to "take the leap" and give up car ownership for good.

Within months, we began documenting this newfound freedom, mobility, and simplicity via words, photography, and film. Perhaps unsurprisingly, having to spend less time commuting by car, circling to find that coveted parking space, or contributing to the congestion in our city effectively afforded us more time to share our stories. Those active forms of transport inspired us and fueled our creativity, and they continue to do so today.

Over the past eight years, this work has taken us to places we never could have imagined, as we garnered a global audience on social media and ended up speaking about the (many) triumphs and (few) challenges of our "car-lite" lifestyle in cities as far away from home as Montreal, Quebec; Philadelphia, Pennsylvania; and even Auckland, New Zealand. It also provided the basis of Modacity—our fledgling multi-service creative agency that now works with a variety of public and private partners around the world.

In December 2015, after several years of writing about North America's emerging bike cultures, we walked into the office of our editors at *Daily Hive* with an ambitious proposal: a five-week, five-city tour of the Netherlands during the summer of 2016, to gather their inspiring cycling stories and share them through words, photography, and film. To our immense surprise, they immediately said "yes," and with the help of some additional corporate sponsors and a modest crowdsourcing campaign, we set off with our two children on the trip of a lifetime.

Those five weeks were nothing short of life changing as we pedaled along Rotterdam's stunning Erasmus Bridge and the Maastunnel, Eindhoven's awesome Hovenring and Van Gogh Path, Amsterdam's bustling Vondelpark and Rijksmuseum, Utrecht's vibrant Vredenburg and Biltstraat, and Groningen's impressive "smart routes" and car-free city center. We also had the immense privilege of sitting down with many local experts, such as the Urban Cycling Institute's Meredith Glaser, Dutch cycling ambassador Mark Wagenbuur, *Cycling Cities: The European Experience* co-authors Ruth Oldenziel and Frank Veraart, and the University of Amsterdam's own "Fietsprofessor" Marco te Brömmelstroet.

Upon our return to Vancouver, we wrote a series of feature-length articles about each city we visited, an exercise that was equal parts rewarding and frustrating. The latter came from having to reduce so many jam-packed days of amazing experiences, several hundred years of socioeconomic history, and the many fascinating characters we met along the way into just 1,500 words. A tremendous amount of the material we had initially hoped to cover was left on the "cutting room floor." So, after completing the final story in September 2016, we resolved to assemble a book pitch, which formed the basis for the volume you're now reading.

Of the overwhelming outside interest that drove the crazy journey to this particular point, we can only offer the following explanation: our followers were, and continue to be, intrigued to see a livable, life-sized city through the eyes of one (or four) of its users. This has turned our family's unremarkable day-to-day existence into something truly noteworthy, where the simple act of moving around our city is a memorable, shareable, and joyous experience.

From a more personal perspective, our decision eight years ago to go "car-lite" had a tremendous effect on our relationship as a family. Raising children is a challenging endeavor, and dedicating ourselves to more active modes of living certainly adds to that. But we have found that making most trips on foot or bike has led to very meaningful conversations with our children, because we focus more on them and not on what is happening through a windshield. It is an outcome we never could have anticipated, but we have a better understanding of their experiences and developing personalities, simply because of the human scale at which we travel through Vancouver.

At the end of the day, our family doesn't identify ourselves as "car-free," nor are we stubborn radicals determined to save the world. We chose simple means—walking or cycling—for the majority of our daily trips because they are the most practical, efficient, and enjoyable ways to get from A to B. More families like ours will choose these healthier, happier means once our cities make them not just safe and convenient, but also delightful.

Chris and Melissa Bruntlett
January 29, 2018
Vancouver, British Columbia

INTRODUCTION: A NATION OF *FIETSERS*

From Seattle to Sydney, from Los Angeles to London, and in car-clogged urban centers around the world, the humble bicycle is enjoying a second life as a legitimate form of transportation. Ubiquitous on city streets for the first half of the twentieth century, and then abandoned in favor of the private automobile by urban planners and the public for the second half, city officials are suddenly rediscovering the bicycle as a multi-pronged solution to many of their most acute twenty-first-century problems.

Faced with immense problems such as widespread obesity, traffic congestion, climate change, class inequity, social isolation, and budgetary constraints, decision makers have brought this nimble machine back from near-extinction to confront these daunting challenges head-on. There is, however, one nation that kept calm and pedaled on after the Second World War, even as virtually everyone else succumbed to the romance of the motor vehicle. This is a country where the prime minister and members of the royal family are regularly spotted on two wheels: the relatively small Northern European Kingdom of the Netherlands.

The Danish capital of Copenhagen may get a great deal of press and endless plaudits as the world's foremost cycling city—but quite frankly, that is as much a product of effective marketing as a result of effective policy. This tremendous hype also neglects the world's foremost cycling nation, just a few hundred kilometers to the southwest, the only country in the world where the number of bikes (22.5 million) exceeds the number of people (18 million). It is a country where citizens take 4.5 billion bicycle trips per year, during which every man, woman, and child pedals an average of 1,000 kilometers (620 miles), and adolescents cycle almost 2,000 kilometers (1,240 miles).

Consider this: in December 2016, when the City of Copenhagen loudly declared to the world that bicycles outnumbered cars on its streets for the

first time in decades, the milestone was amplified by every major news out-
let in the world. Six months later, a report by sustainable-mobility consultants Excellent Cities quietly revealed that the same was already true in 202
different cities and towns across the Netherlands (for trips under 7.5 kilometers—a little under 5 miles). The related infographics did the rounds on
social media and quickly faded into obscurity—a surefire sign that, despite
their incredible success story, the Dutch are rather poor at sharing and
celebrating it.

Bring these amazing accomplishments up in conversation, though, and
one is immediately greeted with the dismissive assertion "That would never
work here," followed by a number of other misguided claims. But the Dutch
don't cycle because their country is flat (if it were that simple, then Chicago
and Winnipeg would be the biking capitals of North America). The Dutch
don't cycle because the weather is nice (and anyone caught in a brutal wind-
or snowstorm blowing off the North Sea will refute that idea). The Dutch
don't cycle because they're morally superior to the rest of the globe (their
electoral flirtations with far-right candidate Geert Wilders should put that
myth to bed).

No, the Dutch cycle because they've built a dense, 35,000-kilometer
(22,000-mile) network of fully separated bike infrastructure, equal to a
quarter of their 140,000-kilometer (87,000-mile) road network. The Dutch
cycle because they've tamed the motor vehicle, with over 75 percent of their
urban streets traffic-calmed to a speed of 30 km/h (about 19 mph) or less.
The Dutch cycle because their government spends an astonishing €30 ($35
USD) per person per year on bike infrastructure—fifteen times the amount
invested in nearby England.

The returns on those strategic investments are myriad and well documented. Safer streets result in far fewer traffic fatalities, with just 3.4 annual
deaths per 100,000 inhabitants (versus 10.6 in the United States), a rate that—
if successfully transferred across the Atlantic—would save over 20,000 American lives per year. And this intelligent and intuitive street design doesn't just
preserve human life. It adds years to it. A 2015 World Health Organization
report predicted the Netherlands would be the only European Union country
to reverse its rate of obesity in the coming years, projecting an 8.5 percent rate

in 2030 (versus 50 percent in Ireland), largely because they've incorporated physical activity into how people get from A to B. Current Dutch cycling levels are estimated by Utrecht University to prevent 6,500 premature deaths per year, saving the economy €19 billion (more than $23 billion USD), about 3 percent of their gross domestic product (GDP). Similar bicycling rates in the United States would save a staggering 125,000 lives each year.

The transportation sector remains one of the largest contributors to greenhouse gas emissions, and thus it represents the lowest-hanging fruit for governments looking to meet difficult carbon-reduction targets in the worldwide fight against catastrophic climate change. The Netherlands demonstrates a clear path forward, with a 2014 World Bank report ranking it in the bottom 25 nations for transport-related carbon dioxide (CO_2) emissions, measured as a percentage of total national production. In fact, Dutch transportation contributes just a fifth of their overall emissions, compared to a third in the United States, which—with 1.9 billion tons of CO_2 emissions in 2016—overtook power generation as the most-polluting sector in the country for the first time in over 40 years.

Then there are the immense quality-of-life improvements that come with prioritizing the bicycle as a mobility device, especially among the young and elderly. A 2013 study conducted by UNICEF found that Dutch kids topped the list for overall well-being when compared to children in the world's 29 wealthiest countries, in part because of their ability to roam freely without parent supervision. Dutch adults, meanwhile, were ranked seventh in a global quality-of-life index presented at the 2017 World Economic Forum in Davos, which considered factors such as affordability, inclusivity, life expectancy, and equality. Canada and the United States, on the other hand, were ranked 13th and 23rd, respectively.

The final and perhaps most compelling piece of this puzzle is the fact the Dutch have proven that a place that works for cycling also works better for driving. For three consecutive years (2015–2017), the navigation app Waze's Driver Satisfaction Index—which analyzes the experiences of their 65 million users in 38 countries and 235 cities across the globe—named the Netherlands as the most satisfying place in the world to drive a car, referencing its "smooth traffic conditions" and "solid road quality."

It may seem counterintuitive, but a key ingredient in creating the world's most enjoyable driving conditions is providing the freedom to leave the car at home. With the ability to walk or cycle for short trips, take a tram or bus for longer trips, and use a fast, accessible national rail system for inter-city trips, the automobile is viewed as a last resort by many Dutch families (despite a rate of car ownership remarkably similar to that of the United Kingdom). With fewer motorists traveling both short and long distances on the country's roadways, space is freed up for those who really need it, such as freight companies and emergency services. In addition to reducing the amount of congestion, this also decreases the need for maintenance due to "wear and tear."

To truly understand how normal and mainstream getting around by bicycle has become in the Netherlands, one must simply reflect on the fact the Dutch language has two different words for "cyclist." The first, *wielrenner* ("wheel runner"), is the hunched and helmeted archetype that dominates both the streets and psyches of most North American cities. *Wielrenners* are the fit and the brave, decked out in brightly colored clothing and safety equipment, and likely wanting a shower and a change of clothes when they reach their destinations. They represent a narrow and prohibitive type of cycling, which, tellingly, makes up only a tiny fraction of the biking done by the Dutch, mostly just for recreation (and not transportation) on a Sunday morning.

The second Dutch term for "cyclist"—*fietser*—is quite the opposite in its connotation. *Fietsers* are riding around in their normal street clothes, at a moderate pace, on bikes with an upright frame, without any sort of reflective or safety gear, particularly head protection. They're not "running with wheels"—they're *walking* with them. They represent a far more accessible, casual, and inclusive style of urban cycling, and they just happen to make up the vast majority of people cycling on Dutch streets. Unfortunately, outside the Netherlands they are in the distinct minority, in part because of inherent structural and cultural conditions that favor the fast and furious over the slow and steady.

Over the past few decades, many traffic engineers in the Western world have settled for dangerous door-zone painted bike lanes and sharrows, even as they pay precarious lip service to a mode of transportation they've never really taken seriously. And those compromises have had obvious impacts on the number and type of people riding bikes in their jurisdictions. But that laissez-faire attitude has changed very quickly as more and more regions invest in complete, comfortable networks of physically separated cycle tracks, traffic-calmed boulevards, and off-street trails, all designed to make traveling by bicycle far easier—and the everyday *fietser* far more commonplace.

As countries around the world look to the Netherlands for two-wheeled inspiration, they'll find a number of critical takeaways, but none more important than this: *Every location is different, and it's never as simple as copying-and-pasting their methods.*

Rotterdam's postwar transformation offers up inspiration for other car-centric cities trying to tame their mean streets, none of which are as famously mean as New York City's. In Groningen, courageous political leadership has been paramount in taming the car, and similar bravery is now manifesting itself in an "all ages and abilities" bike network in the emerging cycling city of Vancouver. In Amsterdam, citizen intervention persisted, narrowly saving their bicycle infrastructure from burial under freeways, and those activists are now inspiring a new generation of Bostonians to demand more. In Utrecht, residents have realized that the goals of a human-scale city and car-first city are mutually exclusive, and similar sentiments are now encouraging San Franciscans to reconsider the role of their own thoroughfares. And in Eindhoven, leveraging cycling has reinvented their city from one of industry to one of technology, and the sprawling Prairie city of Calgary now hopes to follow in its tracks. And beyond such lessons regarding infrastructure and policy, a significant cultural shift is also needed, one that seamlessly integrates the bicycle into everyday life.

Knowing that the work of the world's foremost cycling nation is never done, the Dutch are now looking even further afield, embracing new ideas and technologies to continue decreasing the number of cars, vans, and trucks on their roadways. Electric-assisted bikes, cargo bikes, and cycle superhighways are being implemented and incentivized, as well as parking solutions that better connect bicycle and rail travel, all in the hopes of making the single-occupant vehicle a thing of the past.

But one size won't fit all, and—like Rome—the Dutch cycling utopia wasn't built in a day. It took over 50 years of incredibly hard work, a bit of good fortune, and some forward-thinking decisions that extended far beyond the current political cycle. Only because of all these factors do residents of the Netherlands enjoy a society that runs on the power of the bicycle, and the countless benefits that such a society brings to everyone, whether they choose to ride or not. By building superior places to cycle, the Dutch have also built superior places to live. And the entire world has a great deal to learn from their story.

01 STREETS AREN'T SET IN STONE

---

*Rotterdam will be a beautiful city. It will be spacious, it will
have the elegance of a metropolis: the speeding traffic, the broad
boulevards, all the tall buildings will generate a sense of bustle
that blends harmoniously with modern life. It will not be easy-
going, but today we would prefer to see a row of gleaming cars
than a carriage full of old ladies. Rotterdam will be our city, the
city of twentieth-century people.*

— REIN BLIJSTRA
Letter to the Het Vrije Volk *newspaper, November 13, 1952*

Few contemporary cities have endured the trauma of having their entire
urban fabric erased overnight, but that was precisely what befell Rotterdam
on May 14, 1940. In an ultimately effective attempt to shock the Dutch government into surrender at the onset of the Second World War, a ninety-plane
wing of the *Luftwaffe*, the feared German air force, bombarded the city with
87 metric tons (96 US tons) of explosives, tragically killing nearly 1,000 residents, making another 85,000 homeless, and fully leveling all but 12 buildings within the 600-acre city center.

Prior to that catastrophic event, Rotterdam was a typical fine-grained
Dutch city—founded in 1340—with narrow and cobbled streets, low-rise
buildings, historic canals, and a red-light district. But, like any other city, it
wasn't without its challenges. While the port of nearby Amsterdam thrived
during the seventeenth century, as can be seen in the city's elegant and orderly

urban structure, Rotterdam's harbor didn't experience its own economic boom until the Industrial Revolution, over 200 years later.

"As a result, there were factories in the middle of the city, and a lot of pollution," suggests Dr. Michelle Provoost of the Rotterdam-based research collective Crimson Architectural Historians. "People lived right in the middle of that industrious climate, in small, dark, and unhealthy homes. There was a huge dissatisfaction with this pre–World War II city that we would probably not understand today."

That discontent with a mixed, messy city—especially among the ruling classes—manifested itself in an "urban renewal" plan similar to those seen in North American cities. As Provoost points out, planners in Rotterdam were already devising radical transformations to unclutter and "sober up" the city, even before the bombs fell: "They were tearing down huge parts of the inner city to create more space for urban traffic. The bombardment came as a shock, of course, and it was a disaster. But also at the very same moment some people were saying: 'This is a gift from God.'"

Postwar rebuilding efforts were fast and furious, embraced by planners, politicians, and city officials as a once-in-a-lifetime opportunity to modernize Rotterdam, untie its problematic "knots," and redesign it around society's newly mass-produced panacea of economic prosperity and personal mobility: the private automobile. They believed that the bike as a mode of transport—extremely common in this working-class city—would meet its necessary and inevitable demise. Rather than share the road with cars, Rotterdammers would trade in their pedals for shiny new motor vehicles.

"The story in Rotterdam is, only a few days after the bombing, the planners had the first renewal plan ready, as if they were waiting for the moment to turn it in a very modern city," claims Jeroen Laven, partner at the Rotterdam-based urban planning firm STIPO. "They were saying, 'Now we have the opportunity to prepare for this modern age with more cars, and solve a lot of the problems of the old city.'"

As in New York, and countless other places enthralled with Robert Moses' unsympathetic vision of the future, the old streets and canals were paved over with wide, multi-lane boulevards and long blocks. High-rise buildings with huge parking garages were prescribed and built, and a strict zoning

Figure 1-1: Once the German bombs had stopped falling, the fires were extinguished, and the debris was cleared, little was left of Rotterdam's city center. (Credit: Wikimedia Commons)

code separated the city's core components: work, commerce, and living. The technocrats touted these concepts to a skeptical public as a matter of inevitable progress, on a scale and scope far more familiar in North America than anything seen in Europe at the time. "It was very effective, this myth that Rotterdam would reinvent itself and rise from the ashes like a phoenix," says Provoost. "In the juxtaposition between Amsterdam and Rotterdam, that is the identity of the city: dynamic, changeable, and resilient."

Aided by US president Harry S. Truman's Marshall Plan—which provided the Netherlands with over $1.1 billion (USD) in financial aid to rebuild the roads, railroads, bridges, and factories that had been destroyed—the rebuilding necessitated by this "gift from God" proved in some ways to be fortuitous. For instance, it allowed Rotterdam to modernize its harbor facilities, making it one of the first to invest heavily in the freshly introduced concept of containerization and establishing Rotterdam as the world's busiest port (until it was eventually surpassed by Singapore and Shanghai in 2004). As a consequence, Rotterdam also evolved into a multinational business hub, with many shipping, pharmaceutical, banking, energy, and chemical companies strategically locating their headquarters on the Maas River.

For over 20 years, this unparalleled experiment in car-first planning continued unchecked, until the early 1970s, when many Rotterdammers started to realize that the reality of the automobile age fell far short of the dream of progress they had been sold. Growing congestion, decreased air quality, plummeting cycling rates, and a plague of road fatalities, particularly among children—all seen as the "cost of commerce" elsewhere—were enough for them to demand a change from their elected officials.

Taking Back the City

"In the beginning of the seventies, all over the Netherlands there was a switch from large-scale to small-scale, from car traffic to public transport, and from the economy to the environment," recalls Provoost. Cities across the country were realizing that the rebuilding of their infrastructural framework, with an emphasis on economic growth, had become unbalanced. Instead of feeling a sense of ownership of their streets, Rotterdammers were left fighting for scraps of space on the sidewalk. They eventually decided it was time to rebalance the scales and take back their city from the technocrats.

And then, in 1973, OPEC announced that the Netherlands—the home of Royal Dutch Shell—was one of five countries to be targeted by an oil embargo, resulting in an abrupt gasoline shortage and compelling the nation's 3 million motorists to reevaluate their relationship with their cars. A dramatic spike in fuel prices forced many to reacquaint themselves with bicycles—the sales of which doubled—which, in turn, resulted in a collective desire for safer streets. This shift was reinforced by the national government's "Car-Free Sunday" policy, announced by Prime Minister Joop den Uyl as he cycled outside his official residence. Suddenly, for one day a week, Rotterdam went completely quiet, and its broad thoroughfares were returned to the public realm. "It opened people's eyes to the incredible amount of space that was reserved for the automobile," submits Provoost, "because suddenly you had these days when you could roller-skate on the highway, which—for everybody—was a real 'wow moment.'"

Laven adds that "It was an instant in Dutch history when you started noticing you can't take certain things for granted." According to him, though, something more pragmatic drove Rotterdammers' rejection of the modernist ideals that had been implemented. During the eighties and nineties, Amsterdam and Rotterdam both had 80,000 people working in their city centers. In Amsterdam, however, 80,000 also *lived* in the center, whereas only 20,000 lived in the center of Rotterdam. This made the inner city feel completely empty, especially on evenings and weekends. As more and more individuals started to complain about how boring the inner city was, the conversation began to shift. Rotterdammers began asking out loud, "How can we finish the inner city? How can we improve it?" They demanded to see accessible housing, vibrant public space, and more day-to-day functions return to the downtown, instead of seeing the life drain from it at the end of the work-week. Everyone had clearly been romanced by images of crowded Manhat-tan sidewalks, which never actually materialized in Rotterdam because of the problematic way the zoning code had pushed housing out of the city cen-ter. "The inner city became windy and uncozy, and people were very critical of it," reveals Provoost. "In the seventies, this critique came to a pinnacle, leading to the narrowing of streets to make them cozy again."

Thus began three decades of reversing the damage done in the name of urban renewal and retrofitting streets designed "according to the demands of modern fast traffic" to a more human scale. Wide, grass-lined boulevards were established down the center of many arterial roads, and these were integrated into a fast, frequent tramway system that would never get stuck behind single-occupant vehicles. Sidewalks were widened, and generously proportioned one-way cycle tracks were built on both sides, completely sep-arated from automobiles. Perhaps more importantly, the zoning code was relaxed, housing was reintroduced to the city center, and thousands of new apartment units were built.

By building complete streets and complete communities, Rotterdam reversed many of its problems and its citizens' lives were all the better for it—thus reminding cities that the design of their streets aren't set in stone, nor are they frozen in time. Even the most car-centric city can be adapted for walking, cycling, public transit, and public life.

It wasn't just the city center that benefited from these retrofits. "In Rotterdam," Laven explains, "because of the bombing, the good cultural spots were spread out around the city, so you needed a bike to get from one place to another." Hence, the city's 4-meter- (13-foot-) wide cycle tracks eventually stretched to every corner. "The challenge was to connect the empty spaces at street level between those spots. So, if it were made attractive enough, you would cycle as in other cities you would walk." Provoost agrees wholeheartedly: "In Holland, cycling has been part of the culture, part of the way we get around, for such a long time that it's deeply ingrained and has been for at

Figure 1-2: The broad Rotterdam thoroughfare of *Stadhoudersweg* receives a "road diet," complete with cycle tracks and a grass median for trams. (Credit: Modacity)

least a century. You don't have to have a helmet or special clothing. It's just a faster way of walking. 'Pedestrian plus,' you could say."

Rotterdam also made a point of building streets that were accessible to all ages and abilities. "We took some big steps to make it safe for children and elderly people to cycle," Laven says. "I have a feeling that we do better there than quite a lot of other cities." He credits this to the modernist influence, where wide avenues can easily be transformed into safe, pleasant streets with cycle lanes. Cycling's modal share in Rotterdam may be low by Dutch standards—about one in four trips are made by bike—but this would be an enviable rate anywhere else in the world, and it's growing quickly as officials work tirelessly to make the cycling experience more relaxed, intuitive, and seamless.

"Rotterdam has had this one advantage over other Dutch cities, being that there is much more space in the urban infrastructure," continues Provoost. While for many of its counterparts—especially Amsterdam—the increasing number of cycle lanes has come at the expense of the walking realm, Rotterdam enjoys a luxury uncommon in traditional European cities: "Here the bicycle infrastructure has been carved out of the car infrastructure, because that is possible. And that is an ongoing process. The City is continually finding more space for bicycles and pedestrians," she says, pointing to new plans for the *Coolsingel*, the main arterial road in the center, which was recently redesigned to lose half its car lanes and replace them with trees and sidewalks.

"What we are really grateful for, at this moment in time, is these North American–sized buildings and urban fabric," concurs Laven. "They give you so much space to improve the city. There are people who move from Amsterdam, and what sticks out here is that there's so much sky. You can see it everywhere. The sky is a symbol of opportunity. That really gives a lot of energy that this is a city of possibilities."

Seeing the City at Eye Level

Viewing Rotterdam as a place with limitless potential, Laven and his colleagues at STIPO have spent recent years studying the importance of repairing the urban fabric at ground level. After the war, the "blank canvas" created by the bombing removed certain architectural constraints—such as height, color, and context—leading to some stunning and innovative experiments with the built environment.

"Rotterdam is known as a place where you can see all of the postwar experiments that ever happened in architecture," he says. "The attitude was 'we have to rebuild the city. We have to do it fast because there is a shortage of housing. But it's okay if we make some mistakes, because we'll just demolish them and start again.'" This redesign placed an emphasis not on traditional streetscapes of the past—with buildings lining them—but on single objects. They built stand-alone theaters, hotels, and train stations, which, being isolated, broke the continuity of the street façade.

While some of these architectural experiments have helped shaped a rather spectacular skyline—including Piet Blom's Cube Houses, MVRDV's Market Hall, Rem Koolhaas's De Rotterdam, and the spectacular Centraal Station—most managed to fail Rotterdammers at the most basic level. The ground floor, or—as STIPO refers to it—plinth, makes up only 10 percent of a building, but determines 90 percent of the building's contribution to the experience of the urban environment. Simply put, the plinth is where life happens, and where pedestrians and cyclists experience the city and those people around them.

Recognizing these gaps in their streets, the City of Rotterdam approached STIPO about joining with the City administration to develop a plinth strategy for the city center, the very first of its kind in the world. This document also formed the basis for *The City at Eye Level*, a collection of nearly 60 stories written by professionals from such varied settings as Toronto, Tokyo, Mumbai, and Johannesburg. The free e-book—edited by Laven and three of his peers—outlines best practices on how to make great, human-scale streets by carefully considering their six key elements: the façades, buildings, sidewalks, streets, bikeways, and trees.

Laven's work is indisputably informed and inspired by his daily travels around Rotterdam perched on his upright bicycle, which he equates to a slightly faster and more efficient form of walking. He likens his wheels to an extension of his body, a sentiment to which many Dutch people can relate, and is firm in his belief that pedaling a bicycle is like taking a pleasant stroll through the arteries of his beloved city.

"Giving space to pedestrians and bikes is the same. You need to give people enough space to stroll in a safe way, and just enjoy the city as it is. For the Dutch, that's completely normal," he declares. That plentiful space is what will keep Laven and his family living in Rotterdam for the indefinite future: "It's a great city because there's space to live. There's space to experiment. There's space to cycle, too."

Leading an Urban Revolution

Experiencing the city at eye level, and then planning accordingly—as Rotterdam has done for the past half century—is a strategy increasingly applied to streets around the world. A new crop of "plangineers" are recognizing that in order for cities to be successful for the people that live in them, their approach needs to come from the ground up, and not from above, as their modernist predecessors tried to do and failed.

One of the more lauded and high-profile examples of this new attitude can be found in a former Dutch colony that is now the seemingly untamable global capital—New York City, formerly New Amsterdam. The "City That Never Sleeps" undertook a dramatic transformation that is largely credited to its darling—at least in transportation planning circles—Janette Sadik-Khan, transportation principal with Bloomberg Associates, chair of the National Association of City Transportation Officials (NACTO), and co-author of *Streetfight: Handbook for an Urban Revolution.*

"My education of the streets started at a very young age, walking throughout the city with my mom," Sadik-Khan reminisces. "When you look at the street from the foot up, it's a very different perspective, and that really informed my ideas around city building and transportation." Growing up as a New Yorker, she spent her childhood experiencing her city, in all its glory and failings, at the ground level, which ultimately informed her professional journey, beginning as an employee for the New York City Department of Transportation (NYC DOT) under Mayor David Dinkins.

But it wasn't until her return after 15 years in the transportation field at the national and international level—including a stint advising President Bill Clinton—that she was given the chance to bring out the best in the streets she had grown up with. In 2007, as the newly elected mayor, Michael Bloomberg, began putting together his administration, Sadik-Khan successfully lobbied for the position of transportation commissioner. Her aspirational plan included a bold vision to bring the best ideas from around the world to the 6,300 linear miles of New York City streets—an astonishing 25 percent of its surface area—and shape this diverse metropolis for the better.

From day one, she challenged the status quo, asking her engineers, "Why can't we do something like that here?"—referring to examples of rapid bus lines in Bogotá, separated cycle tracks in the Netherlands, and the new public space being added to the centers of a growing number of cities. "The common response I got," she says, "was that the issue was mostly political and cultural, but didn't have much to do with engineering."

Luckily for Sadik-Khan, she had the political climate on her side. Mayor Bloomberg was dedicating his tenure to PlaNYC, a sustainability agenda that studied what needed to be done to make New York City become a better functioning place by 2030. The farsighted plan, anticipating an influx of a million more people, aimed to improve New Yorkers' quality of life by improving the quality of their neighborhoods and business districts. PlaNYC "raised some pretty profound questions for the Department of Transportation, and there was no way to get there without rethinking our streets," says Sadik-Khan. "Fortunately we didn't have to reinvent the wheel." By looking at global examples, Sadik-Khan and her team developed their own "New York Way" of designing their streets to ensure they would be safe for people whether seven or seventy.

At that time, global information sharing around urban development was still in its infancy, with Twitter barely a year old and the most popular urbanist blogs yet to reach a mainstream audience. For many of the New Yorkers whom Sadik-Khan was trying to reach, images of cycling utopias such as Amsterdam were unfamiliar, and they were understandably skeptical of any proposed change to the streetscape.

Sadik-Khan's approach to this was pragmatic. "The point isn't that there is a 'Dutch' bike lane," she says, "it's really more of an approach that you're bringing. The Netherlands wasn't always this way—it was created and evolved—and that was very inspiring to me." To change the hearts and minds of residents, these upgrades couldn't be a cut-and-paste duplicate of somewhere else—they had to be created in New York. Her department would install over 400 miles of "Made in New York" bike lanes, and later launch Citi Bike, the single largest public bike-sharing scheme on the continent.

Figure 1-3: A protected bike lane along Brooklyn's Prospect Park, once referred to as "the most contested piece of land outside the Gaza Strip." (Credit: Doug Gordon)

Many of these upgrades were made possible simply by unlocking the hidden potential found in most city streets. For example, traffic engineers have historically designed automobile lanes to be 12 feet in width—even in an urban setting—despite the typical Toyota Camry being just 6 feet wide. This standard is meant to provide a safety "buffer" typical of rural highways, where vehicles are moving at much faster speeds. By revisiting some of those design decisions, such as reducing lane width to 9 or 10 feet, Sadik-Khan and her team were able to find additional room for wider sidewalks, protected bike lanes, and generous bus stops. Fulfilling this potential meant a much more effective use of space along these corridors, moving a greater number of people in a quicker and more secure manner.

Armed with the knowledge that half the population would be suspicious of the government arriving and saying, "We're here to help," and the other half tired of grand plans that might never come to fruition, Sadik-Khan used a fresh "tactical urbanism" strategy to bring about change in a provisional and cost-effective manner. A growing practice among planners and advocates, *tactical urbanism* is the act of quickly transforming an existing space, using inexpensive materials, to temporarily create a more welcoming environment for walking, cycling, or public life.

Despite early skepticism from the media and the public, by the end of her six-year reign as transportation commissioner, Sadik-Khan became renowned for lighter, quicker, cheaper projects. Her team would redesign a space overnight with some paint and planters, creating pop-up bike lanes and reclaiming public spaces from cars, the most notable example being the now-permanent plaza in Times Square—once a noisy, car-choked, and dangerous destination, now a cherished legacy of Sadik-Khan's tenure.

"I think we were able to push back against the cynicism and challenges by moving quickly and showing New Yorkers something they could touch and feel instead of just arguing about it, and that these projects were a good idea," she insists. But it was about more than just seeing the plans in action. "[The pilot projects] gave us something to measure, and that went a long way to convince some of our biggest skeptics that the program was working, turning them into our biggest supporters."

Mayor Bloomberg's motto was, "In God we trust. Everyone else bring data." That's exactly what she did. After implementing the highly contested protected bike lanes along Ninth Avenue, retailers who had insisted that the lanes would be the death of their business instead saw a sales increase of 49 percent. In the Bronx, along the route of the first of seven rapid bus lines created during Sadik-Khan's tenure, sales shot up 71 percent. As for the plazas, one of the most dramatic increases happened at the small de facto parking lot—and first pop-up plaza—on Brooklyn's Pearl Street, at the foot of the Manhattan Bridge. By simply applying paint, purchasing some planters, and bringing in tables and chairs, the NYC DOT completely transformed the space, and retail sales went up by a whopping 172 percent.

"We were able to show that the better we design our streets, the better it was for business. Having that data can really change the argument from anecdote to analysis," Sadik-Khan points out. By having evidence-based studies to back up the program, the NYC DOT team were able to go to other neighborhoods and communities, show the data, and completely change the tone of the debate. Nowadays, the demand by citizens and businesses alike for bike lanes, parklets, and plazas are off the charts. New Yorkers have seen that such amenities work, and they have watched as life went on as usual and their city became a more vibrant place to live, work, and play.

Business development associations are now teaming up with the City to participate in the Street Seats scheme, in which they transform old parking spaces into places with seating and then commit to creating a well-maintained and supervised program of regular activities. In addition, more than 75 plazas have been created as a part of this innovative arrangement, with local businesses contributing to the upkeep of the new spaces. "When you measure the streets and see a lot of that economic development, there's really nothing more powerful than that," Sadik-Khan suggests, referring to how cities can use data to win the favor of businesses, often the fiercest opponents to such change.

Since stepping down as transportation commissioner in 2013, Sadik-Khan has turned her focus to sharing her knowledge and expertise with cities around the world in order to help them develop their own methods for improving their streets. "The point isn't that there's just one approach," she insists. "I think it's fascinating to see cities learning from one another, and tailoring what they're seeing in other places to their own streets. It's what we're seeing all over the world. It's ignited a different kind of revolution on our streets, one that prioritizes putting people at the top of the transportation hierarchy." Sadik-Khan even admits that she takes delight in watching ambitious mayors compete with one another to make their city "the best."

As the chair of NACTO, she helps the organization provide guidance to its members, enabling and supporting the innovation now taking place in cities across the United States, Canada, and Mexico, and giving them the blueprints they need to get started. In 2017, NACTO's Global Designing Cities Initiative launched the first-ever Global Street Design Guide, giving cities on every continent access to the same transformative tools. The guide was adopted by 35 different cities and 19 nongovernmental organizations in just the first six months after publication. "That's what it's all about," Sadik-Khan emphasizes. "Sharing ideas. That's key to successful cities in the twenty-first century—creating a network of experienced planners and engineers who share ideas of what works on their streets, what doesn't, and why."

Ten years on, Sadik-Khan also believes that, with the explosion of global communications, it's easier than ever to import ideas and strategies from across the globe for how to build streets that work for people. A new crop of passionate urbanists has emerged, using social media as a powerful tool to share what they've been doing. She is now seeing New York City's influence in places like Addis-Ababa, Mumbai, and even in already forward-thinking cities such as Rotterdam. While federal governments seem to be slower to implement large-scale change, citizens and municipalities are more than ready to take up the challenge, and Sadik-Khan couldn't be happier with how her legacy is inspiring a genuine urban revolution. "Right now," she says, "cities are doing it for themselves, and that's a great thing."

Bringing the "JSK Approach" to Rotterdam

Back in Rotterdam, the desire to reinvent their public realm remains as strong as ever. In fact, inspired by Janette Sadik-Khan, the municipality is looking to accelerate change through strategic projects in their own city center. Their newest mobility plan focuses on shifting citizens out of their cars while providing more room for walking and cycling. To complement that work, officials have developed a "City Lounge" strategy (implementing pop-up terraces like those in New York) in an attempt to breathe life back into a historically hollow center.

These planners recognize that, in Rotterdam as in other cities, it is as important to look outside their borders as within, to learn what works best when reshaping their streets. Looking at places like San Francisco, Bogotá, and Paris, and even borrowing New York's "JSK approach" (a shorthand lovingly adopted in urban planning circles), they are bringing people back into the heart of Rotterdam, one pilot project at a time.

José Besselink is an urban planner who grew up in the suburbs of Rotterdam, later moving to Utrecht to attend the university. She now commutes daily from there by train to work for the City of Rotterdam, where she has been improving her childhood home for the past decade. Over the last five years, her work has been heavily focused on the "City Lounge" strategy and inner-city development, and she freely admits that much of her inspiration comes from Sadik-Khan's work across the Atlantic. "Even in Rotterdam, change is hard, so we use pilot projects to alter the mental map of citizens and entrepreneurs," Besselink explains. She and her team want residents to rethink how public space can be more inclusive. They have implemented their own "Made in Rotterdam" streetscape and street furniture while reducing on-street parking to make greater use of the large number of underutilized parking garages in the city center.

As Provoost and Laven noted, after the bombing during the Second World War housing was relocated outside the city center to the surrounding neighborhoods. Besselink now focuses on bringing residents back into the core. "Densification—or welcoming more inhabitants—is one of the main goals of the 'City Lounge' strategy," she notes. "Because there were a lot of new building projects, we built a few extra [underground] parking garages to facilitate parking for these new buildings, and to help us create a more attractive public space above ground." To attract average citizens, including families, back into the downtown core, it is vitally important to build vibrant parks and plazas that function as their back garden. This is why the area around the Lijnbaan—which, when it opened in 1953, was the world's first pedestrianized shopping street—has experienced the highest rate of densification. Rotterdammers want to live in connected places, with access to retail, dining, and public spaces that aren't diminished by expanses of surface parking.

In response to this demand, the City has committed to an ambitious target of reducing on-street parking by 3,000 spaces, a third of the total supply. Many of these spots are removed in the conventional way: redesigning streets to prioritize walking and cycling. But in order to accelerate change, they have incorporated the goal into the "City Lounge" investment program, which works with businesses to create pop-up terraces in the summer months. Merchants apply for permits to take over street parking spots, which become extensions of their storefronts—increasing patio space, establishing outdoor shopping areas, or just creating good places to stop and rest.

Because of its grid-like pattern of wide streets, Rotterdam is known in the Netherlands as a "car city," but Besselink thinks they have finally started to shed that image. "We are at an interesting time because we are in the middle of change, and a lot of people are still attached to their cars. I would say it would have been fair, looking back. But we are in the midst of a moment where this is all changing." She points out that over the last 10 years, the number of people cycling in the city has increased by 63 percent.

The increase in cycling numbers brings a new set of challenges not unlike those seen in Amsterdam and Utrecht: where, for example, do you park all those bicycles? While Utrecht has its own aggressive strategy—one that Besselink makes use of every day on her trip to the office—the approach in Rotterdam has been to stimulate grassroots initiatives to accelerate and complement the conventional "top-down" planning process. Residents in communities across Rotterdam were expressing concerns about the crowds of parked bikes taking over the footpaths, so two years ago, a pair of pioneering individuals decided to work with the City to test a solution in their neighborhood. For a six-month trial, they chose five on-street car parking spaces that would be designated as "bike corrals," suddenly creating room to store 50 bikes. If these corrals didn't help solve the bike parking problem, they could be easily removed. No harm, no foul.

In fact, Besselink reports enthusiastically, "the parking spots were very well used, which allowed us to eliminate not only the original five spaces, but add more in the surrounding neighborhood. We were also able to widen the sidewalks in some areas, and add trees in others. In the end we were able to do more with this pilot than we would have been able to do with a traditional planning process."

Besselink points out that much of the recent work in Rotterdam around improving the public realm has happened through the spirit of collaboration. Instead of developing ideas behind closed doors and releasing them to the public in a high-handed way, the City has openly welcomed input and ideas from their citizens. They are the ones who walk and cycle the streets every day, and they have the best feeling for what is happening at street level, which makes their insight invaluable. "It's not about me sitting at a desk making decisions, but by working with change-makers who are citizens themselves, and are willing to work with us to create change," Besselink explains. While working on their latest mobility plan, the City invited the Dutch Research Institute for Transitions (DRIFT) from Erasmus University Rotterdam to collaborate on workshops tailored to residents. There, locals were invited to bring their ideas for long-term initiatives that could improve the streets and match the municipality's ambitious goals to boost walking and cycling.

During one of these sessions, José met Jorn Wemmenhove, partner from the local urban-design agency Street Makers. Looking beyond Dutch borders for inspiration—this time to Bogotá, Colombia—Wemmenhove pitched to Besselink the idea of bringing a large-scale street fair to the heart of Rotterdam. It would be modeled on Bogotá's weekly Ciclovía event, where 120 kilometers (75 miles) of streets are closed to cars and reserved for pedestrians and cyclists each and every Sunday. Named the "Happy Streets Foundation," the collaboration established three guiding principles for any potential pilot project. One: What is the end goal? Two: What is the transition we want to accelerate? Three: Does it fit within the "City Lounge" policy?

With these standards in mind, they launched their inaugural open-streets event on a Sunday from 9:00 a.m. until 2:00 p.m. in September 2016, opening up one and a half kilometers of streets to the people to enjoy without interference from cars. The event drew about 1,000 Rotterdammers and was deemed enough of a success to ensure its continuation in coming years, expanded to other areas of the city.

After the success of these workshops, Wemmenhove identified the desperate need for a safer pedestrian crossing at the postwar thoroughfare of Westblaak, which acted as a wall carving the city into two halves. If the city was truly committed to improving the safety of their streets, this was ripe for a redesign.

Dubbed the "Creative Crosswalk," the ensuing project was a co-creation of the City, Street Makers, and the local artist collective Opperclaes. "It was a pilot that dignified the pedestrian and gave priority back to them," says Besselink. Vibrant color was added to slow apathetic motorists and enhance the street at pedestrian level. The words "STAND STRAIGHT / WALK PROUD" appear larger than life on the crosswalk as a reminder that pedestrians have the right to the street, and while it is the first pilot of its kind in Rotterdam—harkening to the now-ubiquitous rainbow crosswalks across North America, and Hecho en Casa, an urban intervention and street art festival in Santiago, Chile—the City will be monitoring this intersection closely. If deemed a success, it will be implemented in other problematic areas of Rotterdam.

But of all the tactical urbanism interventions that Besselink has imported to Rotterdam during her tenure, she credits San Francisco's PARKing Day as the start of it all. "It fit the objective of 'City Lounge' so well: create more public space and more green space." Working with Happy Streets, the City simply acted as a facilitator, leaving businesses and residents free to choose their level of involvement. The only limits to the imagination were the City's bylaws, namely no alcohol and no selling.

Each year since 2014, Happy Streets has organized the participants and identified parklet locations to the City. On the day of the event, Besselink and her team travel to each site, feeding the parking meters on the City's dime and enjoying how their fellow citizens transformed a blank canvas—a standard street-parking space—into an inviting extension of the public realm. By 2016, the number of participants had grown to 90, and Besselink is immensely proud to know that she was instrumental in convincing col-

Figure 1-4: A bird's-eye view of Rotterdam's "Creative Crosswalk" pilot project, which spans the wide postwar thoroughfare of *Westblaak*. (Credit: City of Rotterdam)

leagues to try something different, which has grown into such a success in rethinking their streets.

Since the tragic bombing in 1940, Rotterdam seems to have been in a constant state of transition, from an industrial-age European city to a car-centric, modernist port city. It has now spent the last half century changing course yet again, still using the modernist DNA as a local identity but giving the streets back to their rightful owners. While examples of complete street design can be found in their own backyard, innovators like Besselink have shown that looking further afield for inspiration can have a tremendous effect on changing not only the structure of the streets, but also the hearts and minds of its citizens. It hasn't been easy, and it will be some time before other Dutch cities stop referring to Rotterdam as a "car city," but Rotterdammers show no signs of slowing down their efforts. "I think Rotterdam will be a people-orientated place in 10 to 15 years," says Besselink. "I am convinced we are in the middle of a changing era. We only need to convince our local politicians that this is the future of our cities. I wouldn't say that we are a car-free city—but a more people-oriented, accessible city, with room for everybody."

02 NOT SPORT. TRANSPORT.

---

*What is remarkable is that Dutch bicycle makers, for a major
portion of the twentieth century, seized the opportunity
to explicitly not improve the bicycle. From our modern
perspective, so preoccupied with innovation, this may be
difficult to fathom, but it must be understood primarily as an
ingenious marketing strategy.*

— TIMO DE RIJK
Quoted by Zahid Sardar in The Dutch Bike

The story of how the Netherlands became synonymous with cycling would
be incomplete without a closer look at the simple machine that inspired it at
the turn of the twentieth century: the safety bicycle. Had it not been for widespread, nationwide adoption starting in the 1890s, and the central social role
the safety bicycle played over the next 125 years, Dutch cities would probably resemble their neighbors in Western Europe and across the Atlantic,
with wide streets, very little cycling infrastructure, and corridors clogged
with cars. But just as the Dutch people take their unique bicycle culture for
granted, many tend to forget that the vehicle that helped them achieve international notoriety first arrived on their shores with travelers from across the
North Sea.

"The Dutch didn't innovate at all," reveals Carlton Reid, author, bike his-
torian, and editor-at-large of *BikeBiz*. "The Dutch-style bike as we know it
today is a complete copy of the English-designed standard bicycle." Invented
by John Kemp Starley in Coventry, England, in 1888, the standard—or

safety—bicycle gained tremendous popularity throughout the early 1900s across Europe, including the Netherlands, where its simplicity was ideally suited to the Dutch personality: nothing too fussy, and designed simply to be a practical way to get around town more quickly than by walking.

According to Reid, starting in the 1910s British manufacturers began to create models that were more lightweight; they were no longer interested in the slow, utilitarian nature of the standard bicycle, but rather were looking at new technologies and advancements to improve on their original concept. In the Netherlands, however, the bike stayed exactly the same—so much so that by the 1920s many, including the English, started to forget about its origins, and what was once recognized as the British roadster became what is now known as the Dutch bicycle. And who were the Dutch to correct them? After the Royal Dutch Touring Club (that is, the Algemene Nederlandse Wielrijdersbond, or ANWB) advocated for the establishment of a so-called Dutch bike in their periodical *De Kampioen*, they simply ran with it, and today we think of these black, upright frames being as Dutch as tulips and clogs (both of which, incidentally, were similarly "borrowed" from elsewhere).

"It wasn't that it was boring," Reid says, explaining why the Dutch latched onto the design of the bicycle. "They simply adopted what they saw as a perfect product, that did exactly what it was they wanted it to do." However, one explanation he does offer, especially as regards more northerly—and largely Protestant—towns, is that the plain black *omafiets* ("grandmother bike," characterized by a dropped top tube) or *opafiets* ("grandfather bike," characterized by a straight top tube) suited the Calvinist mindset: simple and not ostentatious. With more working-class populations, northern towns enjoyed higher cycling numbers than did their Catholic counterparts in the south (as they still do to this day), and their joy of cycling just stuck.

The Anatomy of the "Dutch" Bicycle

To understand what continues to make that original design so popular in the Netherlands—and increasingly elsewhere, as photos spread around the world via social media—it's important to look at the basic components that have made it so special.

"First and foremost, what sets a Dutch bike apart is the position you sit in when you're riding—the position the bike is forcing you to take," Reid points out. While most frames force riders to lean forward onto their handlebars, the upright position of a Dutch bicycle is so severe that it appears the rider is sitting on a stool rather than a bicycle. This geometry offers many advantages, including a more relaxed approach to cycling, with less strain on the back, shoulders, forearms, and wrists.

In addition to improving the user's comfort, this vertical posture affords a clear, almost-360-degree view of the people and places around them, improving sightlines, safety, communication, visibility, and sociability. It shuns the idea that cycling should be about speed and sport, making it a much broader, inviting, and more-inclusive activity. It also changes perceptions of how citizens can move around their cities, making urban cycling more appealing to demographics that were traditionally left on the sidelines, including women, children, seniors, and the less physically fit and able.

Figure 2-1: A standard, upright Dutch bicycle makes everyday cycling in regular attire a perfectly practical activity, even when carrying an extra load. (Credit: Modacity)

There are other implications that come with the spread of slower, safer, sit-up bikes, including the use of helmets, which, in recent years, have seemingly become essential in many societies. But such cultural norms were established at a time when fast, forward-leaning cycling was ubiquitous, and safe bike infrastructure wasn't. When drifting along at a jogging pace, in an upright position, on a network of dedicated cycle tracks—as the Dutch have done for decades—the notion of head protection becomes altogether unnecessary. Helmet use in the Netherlands remains remarkably low (0.5 percent of all cyclists) and yet, the nation boasts the lowest rate of bike-related head injuries in the world.

But it's more than just the comfortable riding pose; it's the simplicity of the design—and its influence on Dutch bicycle culture—that sustains the normalcy of cycling in locals and visitors alike. Henry Cutler is a New Yorker who moved across the Atlantic for a job as an industrial designer with Philips Electronics in 2001, and never left. "I was absolutely charmed by the Netherlands and the cycling culture," he reflects over 16 years later. After spending a few years in the northern college town of Groningen—famous for being one of the best small cycling cities in the world—Cutler gave up his day job, moved to Amsterdam, and began work on his passion project. In 2003, he opened Workcycles, his own design and manufacturing company, developing a line of products that applied many of the key principles unique to Dutch bicycles.

"The plan was to sell the world on Dutch cycling," reveals Cutler, knowing then—before the days of Twitter—that he was privy to a wonderful secret. "Nobody seemed to be aware of this unique culture outside of a handful of planners and tourists."

"For the Dutch, it's not a thing to obsess about," Cutler says. They may never admit it, or consider themselves to be "cyclists"—an irrelevant term when the vast majority of the population cycles on a regular basis—but their bikes are special to the Dutch. While a bike may be an important tool, it also has to be able to handle everything life may throw at it. "The typical Dutch bike is like an outdoor dog," he explains. "It's got to be tough, but it's got to be comfortable. It's got to take all kinds of abuse, and it's still got to be ready for you the next day outside, where it lives with all the other bikes. So it shouldn't be too attractive, and yet it's got to do its job."

Considered heavy by North American standards, these workhorse bikes are generally made from sturdy steel that can survive anything, from being knocked over in a high wind, to being tossed aside by the garbage man. They must travel for miles every day, and withstand all of the elements, since most apartments lack garages or storage areas to lock them up in. Cutler describes how most people in the Netherlands will even ride their bikes through bent cranks, misaligned wheels, cracked frames, and worn-out brakes, so each and every component of the bike needs to be able to survive tremendous abuse until the day it finally falls apart.

One of the most striking things for an outsider when looking at a Dutch bike in any shop is how *complete* it is. As has been pointed out, people in the Netherlands are incredibly pragmatic, and they don't want to have to worry about "add-ons" that can overcomplicate the purchase of what will become their daily mode of transport.

Each and every *omafiets* sold in the Netherlands comes complete with the accessories needed to facilitate everyday cycling in regular clothes. Fenders keep the rain and mud off the rider's clothing. A chain casing keeps the chain in near-perfect condition, while protecting trouser legs from pesky grease and tearing. A skirt guard prevents flowing fabric from getting caught in the rear spokes. Coaster (or backpedal) brakes free up one hand for carrying all kinds of useful items, including an umbrella. Dynamo lights run day and night, automatically powered by the turning of the wheels. A frame lock freezes up the back wheel with the turn of a key, providing an added level of security. A bell offers clearer communication on the cycle tracks. Front and rear racks can accommodate any number of functional objects, including crates, baskets, or a passenger; some even incorporate built-in bungee cords. And a kickstand keeps the bicycle from tipping over whenever it is standing still.

These features are also standard on children's bikes, as most kids start cycling solo before they reach school age. Truly, the design is in the details, because the industry knows that this equipment must stand the test of time, and unless bikes can brave the weather and still keep the user dry, they will sit on the sales floor collecting dust. Imagine, for a moment, a car dealership attempting to sell vehicles where lights, locks, horns, and other functional safety items were considered optional "extras."

"It's in the DNA of the Dutch"

The simplicity and practicality of the Dutch bike continues to play a role in the widespread popularity of cycling there, but as Reid explains, it is about more than just the tool they use for the task. "Cycling is a cultural concept as much as it is an archetypal thing. It's the culture—the milieu—that makes Dutch people cycle."

Even after the rest of the Western world started seeing the bicycle solely as a form of exercise and exhilaration, cycling in the Netherlands continued to be an ordinary method of transportation throughout the mid-twentieth century. It would be difficult for a Dutch family today to look back at photographs of previous generations and not see images of their parents, grandparents, and even great-grandparents pedaling away. Conversely, most North Americans would likely have to look back three or four generations to see anything similar, at least when it comes to utilitarian cycling. "In part, it is true that the success of cycling in the Netherlands is due to the separation of modes—the bike paths and the geography. But in part it's also not true," contends Reid, convinced that there is something else at play. "It is in the DNA of the Dutch, in that cycling is handed down through generations. It may not be passed down through genetics, but it *is* passed down through family tradition."

Although cycling in the Netherlands experienced a brief dip in the late sixties and early seventies, where motoring gained a short-lived ascendancy, the Dutch have been riding bikes in large numbers almost since the first one came off the ship from England. Reid suggests that because this tradition was not passed down in other areas of the world, it has been challenging for immigrants new to the Netherlands to adopt the bicycle as readily. As a result, organizations have been working to teach newcomers how to ride a bike and enjoy the myriad benefits of cycling; and while their gradual acceptance of the bicycle as a means of transportation has been a painstaking process, many are hoping that future generations of immigrants will grow up cycling just as naturally as the native Dutch.

The Perfect Bike for All . . . or Is It?

As cycling numbers grow around the world, so too do the number of retailers. But the availability of Dutch bikes outside the borders of the Netherlands is woefully poor, and Cutler spotted an opportunity to use his knowledge of product design and mechanics to expose them to far more people—and to expand the market for them exponentially.

Cutler recalls thinking that "'the world doesn't know about this—about the world of Dutch bicycles, about the world of bicycles as transportation. This is clearly the future. At least it should be, and I should play a role in making that happen.'" From his canal-side shop in the historic Jordaan district of Amsterdam, Cutler and his staff have been designing bicycles that represent all of the values and ideals of the traditional *omafiets*—but for a North American ridership. Cutler believes that many manufacturers, particularly in the United States, have let trends dictate their product offerings, and this has favored quick and easy sales of road, mountain, BMX, and hybrid bikes over complete, practical, Dutch-style bikes that will last their owner's lifetime.

But a change in product offerings is more than just adding upright city bikes to the sales floor. According to Cutler, there also has to be a change in North American cycling culture, one that strips away the bravado of sport cycling. It must be accessible to a broader audience, with a far better understanding of the customer's needs. "When a woman comes in here to buy a bike," says Cutler, "we have to get the details from her: 'Are you a mom? How many kids do you have? How old are they and are you planning on having more?'" These are not questions being asked on sales floors elsewhere, leading to ill-suited purchases of what he calls "the wrong bike for the wrong reason." Sadly, many of these bikes end up collecting dust in their owner's garage, because they are uncomfortable, unpleasant, and unpractical for running day-to-day errands.

Figure 2-2: Hauling five children isn't the Workcycles FR8's precise function, but as Henry Cutler demonstrates, it can indeed be done. (Credit: Henry Cutler)

In what seems to be a standard chicken-and-egg dilemma, Reid offers a differing perspective, arguing that Dutch-style bikes are not stocked outside the Netherlands because the demand doesn't presently exist—and the demand doesn't exist because the bikes are unavailable. "The Dutch bike is very good for their geographic conditions. The majority of people will not cycle up hills, so the heavy Dutch bike isn't practical for them," he insists. And while some smaller North American manufacturers have attempted lighter, context-specific versions of the Dutch bike, and bike-share providers have peppered them across dozens of cities, sales figures aren't sufficient to demonstrate a clear market for them.

"Consumers need to place the demand in order for shops to carry Dutch-style bikes," explains Reid. "Currently these shops are destinations for the people that are dedicated to these types of bikes, which is not sustainable for catering to a wider market." From his perspective, the British and North American markets are completely dominated by recreational cycling, an unfortunate product of decades of hostile street design and "car-centric" policy. Nowadays, the majority of customers periodically strap their bike to the back of their automobile and drive to a trail for some exercise—a sad condemnation of the inadequate on-street facilities in most cities. For better or for worse, the bicycle market is also steered by style, so fashionable colors and models are updated by manufacturers on an annual basis, and consumers are likely looking for something they will replace within three or four years' time.

In order for more people to see firsthand that there is an alternative to the occasional, adrenalin-fueled racing session, retailers must have more than one token city bike on display, and staff must be able to educate their customers on its virtues. But when every square foot counts, dedicating floor space to relatively slow-selling transport cycles makes little sense, and retailers are forced to choose between paying the bills and satisfying a rather small portion of a highly competitive market.

Cutler doesn't accept this rather dismal state of affairs, however. Like many in the advocacy world, he believes it comes down to a lack of education for both the consumer and the retailer, which is why he's very selective when choosing which dealers will represent Workcycles in North America. Only those willing to invest the time it takes to get to know the customer's needs, ask them the right questions, and truly respect everyone who walks through their doors are entrusted with his brand.

When asked whether he has achieved his goal of selling the world on Dutch cycling, Cutler expresses his satisfaction. "We came to the realization a year or two ago that our original mission was fulfilled. Workcycles has been enormously influential in bringing Dutch bicycles to the world," he states proudly. "Now others have picked up the fight for us. The momentum is there, and now we can focus on building a company."

A More Welcoming Retail Environment

Regardless of where the retail market currently stands, if everyday cycling is to flourish outside the Netherlands, buying an everyday bike needs to be made much less complicated than it is now. Most bike shops, for example, greet their customers with the same daunting sight: row upon row of road, mountain, and hybrid commuter bikes, equipped with carbon frames, dropped handlebars, disc brakes, countless gears, and hydraulic shocks. And then there are rows of expensive helmets, cleated shoes, dry-wicking shirts, padded shorts, high-visibility vests, and high-performance socks.

Add to that dynamic an overwhelming and intimidating sales staff that often fail to comprehend that not everyone is looking for a faster, lighter, more high-performance machine. Most retailers conflate the distinct worlds of sport and transportation cycling, to the detriment of the latter. It's the equivalent of a car dealership pushing Formula One–level technology on a family looking for a minivan.

The distinct lack of more-welcoming and less-prohibitive retail environments undoubtedly remains a barrier to the growth of transportation cycling in cities around the world. While industry players focus on competing over their narrow share of the pie—rather than growing the entire pie—the onus will fall on selfless entrepreneurs willing to put passion over profit in order to fill that gaping hole.

Simon and Victoria Firth are the married co-owners of Firth & Wilson Transport Cycles, currently operating out of a 10,000-square-foot former elevator factory in Philadelphia's rapidly gentrifying Fishtown neighborhood. Simon pulls no punches around their shop's *raison d'être*: "We often joke about painting the phrase 'Not Sport. Transport.' in four-foot-high letters on the wall," he admits, only half kidding. Victoria adds, "Unfortunately, the sports mentality is still the driving force of bike shops. But I think they've got to adapt, because people really want these bikes."

The pair opened the shop in June 2013, partnering with Seattleite David Wilson when his wife Rebecka was transferred from IKEA's Delft offices to their North American headquarters just north of Philadelphia, in nearby Conshohocken. During the Wilsons' three years in the Netherlands, David worked in a number of bike shops, even crossing paths with Henry Cutler and Workcycles on several occasions. That short stint definitely influenced Firth & Wilson's emphasis on utility over luxury: "For the Dutch, bike shops are just a way of purchasing and maintaining what you need to get to work and get the kids to school in the morning," claims Simon.

In addition to stocking a number of Dutch brands, including Babboe and Gazelle, their shop boasts a carefully curated selection of city and cargo bikes from Benno, Faraday, Linus, Breezer, Pure Cycles, Xtracycle, and Yuba. Many of these designs are North American variations on the traditional upright Dutch bike—offering lighter aluminum frames, multiple gears, and even electric assist—from companies located in New York, San Francisco, Los Angeles, and Toronto. But crucially, they incorporate all the "bells and

Figure 2-3: The sales floor at Firth & Wilson Transport Cycles, a 10,000-square-foot former elevator factory in Philadelphia's Fishtown neighborhood. (Credit: Modacity)

whistles" needed for everyday cycling in regular attire—including the requisite fenders, chain guards, lights, bells, kickstands, and utility racks—making the purchasing process much less scary and confusing.

According to Simon, a community-focused bike shop is a crucial ingredient in building a bike-friendly city. "Bike lanes are part of creating a cycling city," he explains. "The annual Bike Expo is part of creating a cycling city. And having a great bike shop like ours is part of creating a cycling city." That includes using their space for more than just selling and fixing bikes, as they regularly host art shows, fringe festival events, lectures, film screenings, and charity fundraisers. Philadelphia's growing urban-planning and advocacy scene has even embraced the shop, with 5th Square—the city's urbanist political action committee—renting the space for a number of events.

Simon and Victoria attribute much of Firth & Wilson's success to fashioning a family-friendly setting. Simon happily recounts the dozens of smiling families they've served in their neighborhood since opening their doors in 2013: "Part of the reason I wanted to open this place, was not just to have a bike shop, but to create a more inclusive and welcoming bike scene in Philadelphia." It's the little things, such as finding room in their shop for a small play area—complete with a box of toys—that make bringing the kids along all the more feasible. Visit on a typical Saturday afternoon, and the shop floor will be bustling with moms, dads, and children test-driving multiple bikes, and locals stopping in to drop off or pick up their bikes for repair.

When it comes to building a market for these unfamiliar machines, they really think it is a matter of "seeing is believing." In some instances, Victoria will have a customer walk through the door looking for something sportier, only to be convinced that a Dutch-style city bike is the best fit for their lifestyle. "We do stock some entry-level road bikes and hybrids," she notes. "But we try to show them the alternatives, and in many cases they're really stoked on the three-speed internal step-through frame that's very upright." Despite being used to a faster, more forward-leaning position; the customer's mind is often changed within minutes. "I've seen many instances where, after test rides, people say, 'Oh hey, this is really comfortable. I want this.'"

"Sometimes, you have to show people what they want," insists Simon. Firth & Wilson's best sales strategy seems to be to show these bikes to as wide of an audience as possible, whether it's test driving one in store, renting it for the day, or spotting a neighbor's new set of wheels on the street. "We sell bikes to customers, and their neighbors will ask them, 'Oh, that's cool— where did you get that?'" says Victoria. "These bikes are slowly disseminating through the city, and that's a great thing. It's exciting to hear customers say, 'My neighbor has one of these. I want one.'"

The arrival of Indego, a public bike-share scheme, in Philadelphia has also made this style of cycling accessible to tens of thousands of potential customers who suddenly experience how leisurely, comfortable, and enjoyable bicycling can be. Victoria has noticed a distinct pattern since the Indego program launched in April 2015: "A lot of people have been using the bike-share in town. And they are very upright bikes," she recounts. "And they say, 'I really like that bike, it's comfortable, but I want my own. I'm used to that now. What do you have?' And we're more than happy to help them."

As wonderful as it is to see their market share growing, Simon recognizes that they cannot remain puritanical about one type of cycling, that it would be to the detriment of their business and the community that now depends on them. The end goal isn't to get everyone on a Gazelle, but to empower them to ride on whatever they can afford. "We're just trying to keep people's bikes on the road," he insists. "It's not about everyone having a fancy bike. A lot of people in Philadelphia are poor, and they have cheap $100 bikes, and a lot of new shops will say, 'We're not going to fix that.'"

Firth & Wilson will repair virtually anything that wobbles through the door, particularly if it's someone's primary mode of transportation. "That's part of our success, not being a snob about bikes," asserts Simon proudly. "We might have some $4,000 bikes on the floor, but—to us—your $100 bike is just as valuable."

That isn't to say that swimming against the current hasn't come without its trials and tribulations, but their single biggest challenge—real estate—is one common to virtually everyone living and working in the increasingly unaffordable Fishtown. Paying the rent on such a large space has required some creativity, including subletting some of their square footage to other fledging businesses: "Haley Trikes rents space from us," notes Simon. "I have a frame shop—Hanford Cycles—and I share that space with my friend

Chris, who is a hobby builder. We have a glass blower, a couple of offices, a couple of artists, and an architect in here."

Unfortunately, after watching everything around them sell, the reality of an economy where real estate is worth more than enterprise recently caught up to them. "The building just got sold, and we have three years left on the lease," sighs Simon, but he remains optimistic. "The good thing is, the neighborhood's coming up, and lots of stuff is being built. There'll be plenty of retail space; we just won't have 10,000 square feet of it. We'll move into another, smaller space and we'll continue."

In order to make cycling more accessible to the regular citizen—and not solely the fit and brave—cities are in dire need of trailblazers like Simon, Victoria, and David, who specialize in practical, comfortable, complete machines. There is clearly a latent demand for these types of utilitarian bikes, specifically designed for short trips within an urban environment. As it stands, many of the "interested, but concerned" crowd gets turned away from cycling by the sheer number of specialized bikes they have to sift through just to find one designed for a slow roll to the supermarket.

One thing's for certain: in Firth & Wilson Transport Cycles, Philadelphia has an absolute gem of a bike shop, one that could possibly inspire some altruistic and enterprising citizens to provide a similar hub in their own hometown. Not just as a business opportunity, but as a chance to create a critical resource that will get more citizens—especially women and children—choosing the bike as a mode of transport. "I think the family bike market is growing in Philadelphia," reflects Simon hopefully. "We want to keep providing that place for people to get a bike and try it out."

Electromobility for All

If there's one thing on which manufacturers, retailers, and advocates can agree, it's the potential of the electric-assist bike—or pedelec—to swiftly push city cycling into the mainstream. For over a decade now, e-bikes have been leading a quiet revolution on European streets, where a battery-powered motor has added a new level of mobility, diversity, capacity, and range to what was already an amazingly efficient machine.

Industry insiders will admit that their long-term business plans are centered on e-bikes, with their increased profit margins and servicing costs. Those in advocacy circles are excited about their undeniable ability to close both the gender and age gaps, flatten hills, and remove sweat from the equation, thus addressing many of the barriers to the widespread embrace of cycling as a form of transportation.

As development director of the European Cyclists' Federation (ECF) in Brussels, and president of their Cycling Industry Club—a support group representing 40 of the world's biggest bike companies—Kevin Mayne has his feet placed firmly in both camps. "I think there's not a shadow of a doubt the e-bike is a tool to bring more people into cycling," he affirms boldly. "There are people that perhaps wouldn't cycle without the feeling they get from extra support. So that broadens the number of participants." The other advantage it offers, Mayne maintains, is making journeys that weren't previously conceivable feel possible. An added electric boost offers those who believe they can't cycle due to terrain, temperature, or distance an option to arrive at their destination in a timely manner, feeling fresh and composed.

The science backs up Mayne's claims, with a 2015 study from Norway's Center for Gender Research finding that e-bikes are ridden twice as far and twice as often as traditional, non-motorized bicycles, with the biggest impact on women and seniors. This offers some potentially dramatic changes to transportation patterns within cities, with very real impacts on car ownership and motor vehicle congestion rates.

A 2017 study from the German Federal Environmental Agency discovered that, in an urban setting, regular bikes are faster than cars for trips up to five kilometers. With pedelecs, this radius is increased to ten kilometers, with a marginal difference for distances up to twenty kilometers. "We're no longer talking about the bicycle as a solution for five-kilometer trips," states Mayne. "We're talking about the bicycle as a solution for *most* trips."

There are still some purist voices that denounce e-bikes as "lazy" and "cheating," but Mayne argues that they must be ignored. "If we take the voices of the sporty fit to write the books, we end up with helmets and Lycra, and we end up with no e-bikes. So we have to switch off those voices," he insists. "It's not for you. It's for someone else."

Despite its mostly flat terrain, the Netherlands has emerged as the world's largest pedelec market per capita, with electric bikes making up almost a third of new bicycle sales in 2016. Denmark is a close second, proving to experts like Mayne that infrastructure is absolutely critical, and e-bikes won't sell in significant numbers without a safe space on which to ride them: "The numbers show that countries with good and developing infrastructure have good and developing e-bike markets."

Another crucial ingredient to burgeoning e-bike use is the availability of a safe space in which to store them. "Parking is a huge issue," explains Mayne. "It's a €3,000 [about $3,700 USD] unit, instead of a €150 to €200 unit. People don't want to leave machines of that cost on the street. They want lockers, underground garages, and secure parking at stations." This is one area where the Dutch excel, installing large-scale bike-parking structures within their cities. Known as *fietsenstallingen*, these ample, secure, end-of-trip facilities can be found at major living, working, and shopping destinations, complete with entrance escalators, maintenance facilities, and on-site security staff.

The fact that over 80 percent of e-bike sales in the Netherlands are made to people over the age of 50 demonstrates their unparalleled ability to preserve personal mobility and encourage healthy, active transportation habits well into old age. "There is a need in society to get older, heavier, less fit, and different gender groups active," acknowledges Mayne. He believes the e-bicycle and e-tricycle offer real opportunities in that area, and governments facing ballooning healthcare costs should be thinking about them as game changers: "We're familiar with personalized mobility scooters for the really elderly on the high street. This is a bridge. And it's a lot cheaper."

To see that return on investment, Mayne and the ECF are lobbying governments all over Europe to reconsider their fiscal policies related to electromobility. "If, for reasons of inclusion, you want to make the e-bike part of your solution, they are expensive. So cost is clearly a barrier. Including them in any taxation benefits, or electric-mobility subsidies, is essential," he suggests. While many bureaucrats seem to be betting on a transportation future centered on the electric car, they're ignoring the fact that e-bikes could provide them with a much bigger return on investment.

Figure 2-4: Electric-assist bicycles are an exciting new way to close the gender and age gaps, flatten hills, and remove sweat from the equation. (Credit: Modacity)

Germany provides the most striking example of this, where €1.4 billion ($1.7 billion USD) in electric-car subsidies resulted in just 24,000 units sold as of 2014. Meanwhile, with zero government subsidies, an incredible 2.1 million e-bikes now motor along German streets.

In the Netherlands, a few cities piloted such schemes after national e-bike subsidies were discontinued; currently Utrecht is the only municipality with a permanent program. They now offer grants of up to €1,500 ($1,860 USD) to companies who wish to purchase or lease a pedelec or e-cargo bike for commuting employees or daily business use.

Belgium, on the other hand, is experimenting with a different incentive model, which, for the past six years, has rewarded bike commuters with a €0.22 (27¢ USD) bonus for each kilometer ridden. The average Belgian who cycles to work rode 1,045 kilometers in 2016, making them eligible for a €230 ($285 USD) refund. The e-bike suddenly makes those numbers more enticing. "If you ride a pedelec for a 20-kilometer round trip, you're going to accumulate a lot of kilometers," asserts Mayne, pointing out that such a distance would entitle someone to a €924 ($1,147 USD) annual rebate. "That goes a long way to supporting your bike. So the per-kilometer model incentivizes e-bikes quite well."

Once government agencies level the playing field and provide the necessary incentives, the brakes are well and truly off for the impending e-bike revolution. Many car manufacturers, including Ford and BMW, recognize this as inevitable, so they are developing their own electric bikes for mass production—and they aren't the only major players entering the already crowded market. "When you look at entries such as Bosch, they are a world-leading company in motors and drives," explains Mayne. "They recently established an entire e-bike division—because they think they can make money in this. And they're exporting to China, Japan, and the States."

Mayne's major challenge over the coming years will be to convince these industry players to get behind the ECF's push for safer streets and better bicycle infrastructure in urban centers across the continent: "I'm communicating back to the industry: 'This looks like a magic bullet at the moment, but you need to support us on getting infrastructure built and making roads safer, because the market will plateau.'" In order to fulfill those optimistic business plans, and realize the projected profits, these business owners must help ensure that their customers have great places to ride.

And so, tempering the expectations of manufacturers, retailers, and advocates is perhaps Mayne's most important role, as well as emphasizing the fact that those new users and new trips won't appear without significant investments in active transportation. Getting the basics right has to come first when it comes to increasing cycling rates and sales of new bicycles—whether electric-assist or not. As Mayne points out: "The underlying belief that e-bikes will fix everything is a bit like expecting e-cars to fix everything. It's just another form of the same mobility. So the underlying issues of infrastructure, parking, and safety are not resolved by the technology."

On that front, their daunting and difficult work is just getting started.

03 FORTUNE FAVORS THE BRAVE

Groningen is a true Cycling City. For young and old, the bicycle is the most commonly used mode of transport in the city. In Groningen, cycling is part of our DNA. We are proud of that and we want to keep it that way.

— GRONINGEN CYCLING CITY STRATEGY

Max van den Berg was just 24 years young in 1969 when he decided to throw his hat into the circus ring of municipal politics, mere months after obtaining his sociology degree from the University of Groningen. Despite landing a coveted and relatively comfortable teaching position lecturing on political science and urban-planning issues, dramatic plans to "modernize" his once-fortified hometown—similar to those being executed 250 kilometers (155 miles) south in Rotterdam—convinced Van den Berg to leave the world of academia and commit himself to a higher calling.

After countless discussions with like-minded students, entrepreneurs, and homeowners, Van den Berg realized that someone needed to represent their interests at the political level. "They wanted to bring big roads through the city, and make totally new neighborhoods," he recalls. "Because in the view of the technocrats, these smaller houses and buildings were old-fashioned." As they had attempted elsewhere in the country, planners and policy makers were scrambling to create the ideal conditions for mass motoring, and were prepared to sacrifice Groningen's centuries of history and character in pursuit of the monolithic, monocultural modernist ideals.

According to Van den Berg, a willingness to get his hands dirty developed at an early age. "You could say I was raised—from both my father and grandfather—with the simple idea that democracy is something fairly essential," he claims. "It means every person with conviction can participate in the democratic process, and has the power to change things." Instead of the general feeling of helplessness dominating the public sphere, Max grew up with a hopeful "Yes, you can" attitude, understanding that politics is far too significant to remain simply a spectator sport. Any ordinary citizen can play a critical role and make the change they want to see in their city.

Rather than acquiesce to the demolition of large swaths of his town, in September 1970 Van den Berg ran for, and won, a seat on the city council as a member of the Partij van de Arbeid (PvdA or "Labor Party"), based on a platform opposing these car-centric plans. But rather than latch onto the existing social movements arising in other Dutch cities and towns, he opted to shape his own Groningen-specific solution. "If we don't like this, we don't have to say 'Yes,'" he remembers telling his constituents. "We can say, 'Stop with all these plans and make something new.'"

For his first two years as an alderman, Van den Berg and his allied council members were in the minority, and he behaved as such, raising his objections to these destructive proposals at every available opportunity. "I caused a lot of debate, and that debate created a lot of support. I had support from the traditional labor class, students, professors, and the middle class," he recalls. In the face of that vigorous dissent, four members of the opposition resigned in protest, and Max and five other progressive aldermen were named to a city board tasked with developing the urban and traffic plans. This newly reconfigured board had the support of the majority of the city council, and Van den Berg—at just 26—found himself deputy mayor assigned with the Traffic and Urban Development portfolio.

Max wasted no time taking advantage of his newly secured mandate, drawing stakeholders from the business community, residents' associations, law enforcement, urban planners, students, and cycling advocates, and he gathered them in a room in the Martinitoren ("St. Martin's Tower"), the 700-year-old church located in Groningen's main market square. The goal was to create an alternate proposal for the city center. "We brought in enough coffee, and we said 'no one leaves this room unless you have to do a specific task,'" Van den Berg recollects. "Step by step, we will create this plan. And the technical translation we did in more or less four weeks."

The resulting document, Groningen's now-famous *Verkeerscirculatieplan* ("Traffic Circulation Plan"), proposed dividing the city center to four parts and forbidding cars to cross between those quarters. This made the inner city practically impenetrable with a car, leaving cycling and walking the best ways to get around. The plan didn't completely remove motor vehicles from the equation—as public buses and delivery vans would retain limited access to parts of the core—but it came remarkably close.

The predictable outrage attracted headlines across the country, and Groningen's angry merchants painted slogans on their storefronts, circulated numerous petitions, and demonstrated in large numbers outside City Hall. The local paper ran an editorial referring to Van den Berg as Harry Houdini, suggesting that he was attempting a huge magic trick by making all of the cars disappear. Jacques Wallage, the unfortunate alderman who inherited the traffic portfolio from Van den Berg in 1976, even received several death threats.

Nevertheless, after a 1974 election that saw the PvdA increase its seat count from 11 to 18, the Groningen Council officially adopted the Traffic Circulation Plan, empowered by the consent given to them from a comparatively quiet majority. "That was all done with an enormous amount of public discussion and debate," says Van den Berg. "So people were quite aware of the direction we wanted to go."

It took another two years of preparation before, on September 19, 1977, the Circulation Plan was finally put into action, mainly because Van den Berg and his team understood the importance of getting it right first time around. "I was aware that if you want to change such a thing, you only have one chance," he recalls. "You need political support, and then you can implement it in one day, and you suddenly change the entire system overnight." In a move that predated Janette Sadik-Khan's own lighter-quicker-cheaper approach by three decades, Groningen's city center was radically transformed within just a few hours. City staff scrambled to erect hundreds of provisional barriers and signs forcing motor-vehicle traffic in specific directions, and—

the very next morning—special hostesses were employed to stop and greet frustrated drivers with flowers and informational pamphlets.

The residents of Groningen quickly adapted, and in the following years, city officials turned the temporary treatments into something more permanent, adding landscaping and other materials to make the traffic-calming measures more beautiful and better integrated into the urban fabric. Subsequent studies by the City showed that—despite the protestations of a small, noisy minority—the plan resulted in improved sound and air quality as well as increased retail sales, and it has remained popular with a majority of citizens, who visit the city center more frequently than before.

As a result of this radical civic transformation, Van den Berg was swiftly thrown into the national spotlight and soon was consulting with cities and

Figure 3-1: Accessible only by foot or bicycle, downtown Groningen's Folkingestraat was recently named the best shopping street in the Netherlands. (Credit: Modacity)

towns across the country, whose residents and politicians were desperately trying to find an alternative to the devastating modernist school of urban planning and transportation. "I was invited to Maastricht, Delft, Leiden, Amsterdam, and Rotterdam," he remembers fondly. "For them, Groningen was four years ahead of the rest of the Netherlands. And so, we were an example of what is possible. It helped their imagination. And in politics, you need imagination."

Over a long and varied career in both national and international politics, Van den Berg has been a member of European Parliament, served as chair of the national Labor Party, and sat on the King's Commission as head of the Province of Groningen. Upon his retirement in 2016, he was made an honorary citizen of Groningen, where he still lives and rides his *opafiets*, immensely proud of how he permanently shaped his city for the better.

Today, the Traffic Circulation Plan remains central to Groningen's success as a cycling city on the global stage, where two-thirds of all trips in the city center are made by bicycle—a staggering figure that would have simply been unattainable without Van den Berg's political courage. "In a certain way, it was brave to go ahead," he reflects. "But at the same time we had promised to do it. And we believed you have the right to proceed, if you have the vast majority that we had."

There's no doubt that Groningen would be a very different place today had Van den Berg not made the idealistic—and somewhat naïve—decision to get involved in local politics at such a young age. But, according to him, it was the most effective way to make a genuine impact. "If you only stay a citizen's group, then you usually just end up fighting against politicians," he counsels. "You have to integrate yourselves with the politicians, convince them via knowledge, and sometimes yourselves run for office." And as he demonstrated, age is no excuse: "If you see a wall, when you're young and enthusiastic, you're able to walk through it. And that's exactly what I did."

A City Living on the Power of the Bicycle

In the decades following the execution of Van den Berg's Traffic Circulation Plan, Groningen policy makers went from strength to strength. But somehow—perhaps because of Groningen's modest size and relatively remote location—they've flown under the radar during discussions about the world's best cycling cities, despite boasting a modal share that eclipses those of the established powerhouses, Amsterdam and Copenhagen.

Groningen's profile was raised when filmmaker Clarence Eckerson Jr. of Streetfilms visited in the summer of 2013 and then released a short documentary declaring Groningen to be "The World's Cycling City." The 15-minute film has since been viewed almost half a million times, including once by Tel Aviv native Lior Steinberg, who, at the time, was completing his master's degree in urban planning at Stockholm University. On the strength of Eckerson's inspiring images, Steinberg chose to complete his four-month work term in Groningen, eventually settling there after graduation. He cofounded the *Velotropolis* and *LVBLcity* blogs—a pair of websites and social media accounts dedicated to sharing Groningen's success story with the world—as well as his own urban-planning firm Street Makers, which, among other projects, was instrumental in designing the "Creative Crosswalk" on Rotterdam's Westblaak.

In addition to its historically Calvinist and socialist values—which inspire many wealthy and successful people to choose the humble bicycle over a Mercedes—Steinberg credits Groningen's tremendous number of cyclists to their two-pronged approach to street design, depending on proximity to the inner city. "There are several characteristics that make it a cycling city," he explains. "In terms of infrastructure, it's definitely the complete separation between cars and cyclists outside the city center, and the filtering of cars from getting inside the city center."

Steinberg believes the genius of Van den Berg's plan lies in the fact that you don't notice its existence when you're on foot, bike, or bus. "I've tried to drive in Groningen a few times, and that's where you really feel it," he observes. The end result is that traveling from A to B virtually anywhere in the city is faster by bicycle than by car. "This is something that is quite rare elsewhere. Even in bigger cities where they are investing in cycling and it is catching on as a mode of transportation, it's still often faster to go by car," Steinberg notes. "It might be more expensive, it might be less comfortable, but it's still faster. The circulation plan made cycling faster."

As a result of making cycling the single fastest and easiest way to move around Groningen, local planners have been forced to address a significant problem that many cities would love to have: dealing with the vast number of cyclists during peak hours. "Bicycle congestion" clogs up a number of parts of the city, particularly corridors between the center and the University of Groningen's northern campus.

With one in four of its 200,000 residents attending the two local universities, Groningen's student population has forced the City to find innovative solutions for its busier streets as a way to accommodate a growing number of cyclists. These various solutions include a series of "smart routes": direct, convenient cycle paths designed to get students and staff to the university in less than 15 minutes, without having to put their foot down even once. "Had a late night? Spent too much time in front of the mirror? Use the smart routes," suggests their cheeky marketing campaign via social media, which Steinberg thinks was a brilliant move. "The way they marketed the 'smart routes,' I found it amazing," he says, recalling how students were targeted directly as a way of getting to class on time without having to brave the bus.

Groningen is also one of the first cities to attempt to "solve traffic situations with eye contact," first piloting and then expanding a counterintuitive but highly effective four-way green light for cyclists at 29 different intersections. What sounds like chaos actually creates a calm and orderly ballet between road users, as a dedicated light phase permits cyclists from all four directions to pass through the intersection at once. Steinberg says this was an experiment born out of necessity: "They were trying to find more efficient ways to pass more cyclists in the same amount of time, and this ended up being a bit safer."

However, with as many as 20,000 cyclists traveling certain corridors on a given day, planners are being forced to "think outside the lane" and experiment with the notion of handing entire streets—known as *fietsstraten* ("bike streets")—over to the bicycle as the dominant mode of transportation. Here, street-design features like red-colored asphalt, prominent signage and branding, traffic-calming, and reductions of on-street parking combine to make it abundantly clear that bikes are the main users of the street, and that drivers—as guests—should adjust their behavior accordingly.

Image 3-2: Groningen's newest *fietsstraat*, located on Bessemoerstraat, uses several design features to prioritize bicycles while treating cars as guests. (Credit: Modacity)

The huge number of students proves to be both a blessing and a curse, especially when it comes to behavior on the bikeways. Steinberg points to a study from the University of Groningen that stopped 7,510 cyclists between 1:00 a.m. and 3:00 a.m. on a Sunday morning, 89 percent of who had consumed alcohol, while 68 percent were over the legal limit of 0.05 percent blood alcohol. Nevertheless, although drunk cycling is technically illegal, Dutch officials regard it as a low priority. In a move typical of their sustainable road-safety strategy, they focus on engineering rather than enforcement, designing streets that remove user error from the equation. "By having all those intoxicated cyclists, you really need to make cycling safe, and separate cars from cyclists," Steinberg insists. "Combining drunk cyclists and fast cars is a recipe for disaster. So I do think that having a large number of reckless young cyclists creates the need for better infrastructure."

While Groningen has garnered a reputation in urban-planning circles as a place for testing revolutionary ideas, its politicians haven't always held firm to their convictions. Steinberg points to a 1994 referendum to close the large park just north of the city center to motorized traffic. Noorderplantsoen, up until then, had been home to a busy thoroughfare dissecting the park, and the measure passed by only a narrow margin but could have gone either way. "The results were 51 percent in favor of closing the park to cars," Steinberg recalls. "If now you had a referendum on whether to open that park to cars, it would be 100 percent to keep it car-free."

Steinberg adamantly warns cities against making important planning decisions by referendum, as it allows elected officials to shirk their political responsibility and hand off decisions they deem too controversial to make on their own authority. Despite the slender success of the Noorderplantsoen vote, he thinks the referendum process is often designed to fail: "The people who asked for that referendum were anti-action," he says. "They knew it was easy to mobilize car owners against change, and assumed the quiet majority will not vote." While, to their credit, the supporters of the proposed change did turn up, it would be far better to move forward with a well-informed plan on behalf of the citizens who elected them to make these kinds of decisions.

Forty years on, Steinberg knows Groningen is reaping the fruits of their circulation plan's success. "I've been working with other cities, and Groningen is by far one of the most innovative cities, and one open to change." However, he is quick to remind his other clients that these achievements didn't happen without difficult decisions and short-term pain. "Now if you come to Groningen, it seems like a bicycle heaven," he admits. "But if you look at old pictures, it's really clogged with automobiles. Even if only half of your citizens think banning cars is a good idea, if you're brave enough to actually do it, or you have the political power to do it, in the long run, it pays off."

Like the vast majority of Groningen residents, Steinberg doesn't cycle everywhere for the exercise or for the environment. He rides a bicycle because it's quick, convenient, and comfortable. But above all, propelling yourself on two wheels comes with immense quality-of-life improvements: "When I lived in Tel Aviv, I was driving everywhere," he confesses. "In Berlin and Stockholm, I was using the metro all of the time. Once I moved to Groningen, I really became a happier person, because I cycled every day. Groningen was the first place that showed me a city could live on the power of the bicycle. That's the reason I moved and stayed here."

A Vision for the Future: Principle and Pragmatism

Speak to anyone who lives in the more densely populated southern areas of the Netherlands, and they are likely to bemoan Groningen's remoteness from economic centers like Amsterdam and Rotterdam. Two hours by train from Utrecht, the busiest rail hub in the country, Groningen unsurprisingly remains a smaller city despite its recent acclaim as a "bicycle heaven." But its size is precisely what makes it so special to its residents, who love sharing their secret with visitors from around the world.

This remarkable civic pride is what inspired Steinberg to settle in Groningen after his graduation from the university there, but it is also what has kept its current deputy mayor, Paul de Rook, in the city where he was raised. Elected at the age of 27 in 2014, he is the third-youngest person to hold the position—Van den Berg was just 26—but he brings much of the same altruism and youthful enthusiasm to the post as did his predecessor.

"This is the city where I was born and grew up," he reflects, "and if you are interested in politics and want to change something in your local surrounding, then getting involved with local politics is the best way to do that, in my opinion." De Rook, who started his career in politics when he ran for student council in high school, uses that ambition to build on the work of previous councils, and on the success of the Traffic Circulation Plan. He recognizes that the politicians who came before him had a clear vision of what they wanted Groningen to become, and he now works tirelessly with his peers to make decisions that will continue to sustain and improve it.

But while the focus of the Traffic Circulation Plan was to remove car traffic from the city center, De Rook recognizes that behind those initial plans is really an improvement of both public spaces and livability in general. "You can't make decisions around traffic without having consequences for public space or the livability of the city," he suggests. "You need to incorporate all the views into the same vision for the city." For this reason, Groningen's new vision for the future encompasses a more complete picture of the city, one that combines the values of both principle and pragmatism.

Principle focuses on key factors regarding livability, physical space, and the quality of the environment, and uses a traffic hierarchy to prioritize projects and initiatives. In its simplest form, the traffic hierarchy is: pedestrians over cyclists, cyclists over public transportation, and public transportation over cars. Essentially, the most vulnerable users of the city have priority over the least, and plans are built around ensuring that prioritization.

However, that does not mean building new infrastructure for the sake of it, and this is where *pragmatism* comes in. "We don't enforce this order unless it's necessary, unless there are problems with those fitting together," De Rook explains. In places where modes move together smoothly and without conflict, there is no need for change, with projects only implemented when civic officials identify a problem.

This approach becomes clear during a bicycle ride throughout Groningen, particularly on the "smart routes" that link the university to the center. Before the creation of *fietsstraten*, the most practical and direct routes were becoming increasingly crowded with students and staff traveling to and from school each day, and conflict between modes was intensifying along with the crowding. But now, with *fietsstraten* slowing car traffic and prioritizing bicycles, the whole dynamic of the street has changed. Trips that used to be challenging have become far more pleasant and attractive for those who used to drive their cars but now see the convenience and comfort bicycle travel can offer.

Inevitably, perhaps, a new problem has arisen in the cycling capital of the world. The traffic plan has created such a welcoming city center that its citizens swarm daily to browse the markets and shops, dine in the restaurants, or simply spend time people-watching in Groningen's two main squares. With most of those people arriving by bicycle, the conflicts with buses—currently the only motorized vehicles still afforded access to the center throughout the day (delivery vans are afforded a small window of entry in the morning hours before shops open for business)—as well as those arriving by foot has become a real concern.

Recognizing that many of the trips through the center are not aimed at stopping, but rather just passing through, De Rook and the council are implementing strategies that, as was done with cars in the seventies, provide alternate routes around the core to forestall conflict. "We see that space is becoming too crowded, and its use too intense, so we need to have more accessible public space," he points out. By examining the destinations of the bus routes that traveled through the center, they have identified the routes that can be modified to pass around the perimeter to get passengers to work, school, and home without impeding the vibrant core. To consolidate those routes that provide a crucial link for passengers traveling to the city center, they are devising a shorter, east-west connector route, reducing the size and number of buses. As De Rook explains: "The public space is reserved for pedestrians and cyclists."

With fewer buses getting in the way, the next challenge is the overwhelming number of people on bikes traveling through the city center. Much like they did with the smart routes, the City is providing alternative routes to cycle quickly and easily around the core, thus freeing up valuable space, especially on the weekends. "We thought, 'How can we create an approach that solves the problem in the most-crowded areas at the busiest times?'" notes De Rook. "The answer is to give them an option to go around the city if they don't need to go into it."

For the average North American city striving to increase cycling's modal share, bicycle congestion seems like the best possible problem to have. But as De Rook notes, while the challenges Groningen faces may be different, and even aspirational for other cities, they are challenges nonetheless. With one and a half bicycles for every Groningen resident, bike parking is a consistent and growing issue. As in other Dutch cities, people park their bikes in every available space, whether a rack exists or not. This is creating row upon row of bikes in front of shops, down alleyways, on sidewalks, and in the squares—and taking space away from people on foot.

With a goal of ensuring that the city center be accessible to everyone, including those with limited mobility and parents with strollers, De Rook

Figure 3-3: The number of bikes parked on the streets of Groningen is becoming unsustainable, forcing officials to scramble for solutions. (Credit: Modacity)

and his council know they fall short when it comes to bike parking, and they are working to address it. Partnering with local businesses, they have placed red carpets at the entrance of shops directly adjacent to the street to ensure free access, and restrict where bikes can park. And in order to remove some of those bikes from the sidewalks, they are expanding bike parking away from the busiest areas, as well as working on plans to open a new *fietsen-stallingen* in 2019 to provide space for 1,250 bicycles. This would appear to an outsider to be an acceptable solution, but the demand for bike parking at peak hours (on weekends) is 15,000, so the new garage will be just a drop in the bucket of what's needed.

De Rook views this as an opportunity to enlist additional partners to help fund further bike-parking projects: "For us, it's not really acceptable that you have private business opening up in the center, making a lot of money thanks to the bicycle traffic, but then the government has to invest all the money in the infrastructure. So we try to get them to help as well." He notes that the new *Primark* store—representing a large and popular chain of department stores—will draw many more people to spend money there, most of whom will come by bike and will need a place to park. Teaming up with local businesses to help fund further infrastructure development is mutually beneficial; the City can provide increased space for everyone to arrive at the center by foot or bicycle, creating an inviting space for spending time and money, which is directly transferred back to the businesses in the form of increased profits.

Despite their challenges around space and congestion, Groningen shows no signs of slowing down or resting on its laurels. De Rook explains that they are continually striving to find new ways to make it easier for people to get around by bicycle via new smart routes, and they are even looking at ways to extend their smart routes outside city limits and encourage residents in those areas to travel into the city by bike.

"The real potential for further improvement is with people from villages around the city and them getting to work by bike as well," claims De Rook. He explains that with little effort, Groningen can increase their 61 percent modal share for cycling to 67 percent, simply through the student population. What would be more impressive would be to increase the current 12 percent of people traveling by bike from outside the city, and the City of Groningen is working closely with provincial officials to increase that proportion by 2030. Of course, e-bikes will play a crucial role in any such increase by lengthening the average commute distance from eight kilometers to twenty kilometers with very little additional effort from riders.

Reflecting on the success in Groningen since the implementation of the Traffic Circulation Plan in 1972, De Rook acknowledges that the structure of their city has helped them achieve their impressive status, but he insists it's about much more than that: "You need to provide people with realistic alternatives in order to actually influence their behavior. It's not just building cycling roads and then expecting that everybody will change their traveling behavior. You have to look at it as a system as a whole."

He also offers sage advice for politicians in other cities who are wary of backlash and opposition to bicycle infrastructure plans: get the businesses on board. De Rook encourages engagement and collaboration for devising new plans and strategies, pointing out that often entrepreneurs and business associations can offer help and solutions when it comes to addressing concerns around traffic, the availability of public space, and maintaining economic viability. With business having a greater understanding of proposed changes and supporting such plans, you can reduce the potential for backlash and consequently see greater success. It also helps to focus on the positive; as De Rook says, "We make sure to show what everyone will gain with a new approach instead of dwelling on what they will lose."

Three years into his political career, 30-year-old De Rook is quite pleased with where he's found himself, and he plans to stick around as long as he can. "If you asked me five years ago, 'What would your dream job be when you are 60 years old?,' I would have said deputy mayor in Groningen, and through all sorts of circumstances that happened much sooner, and I think I will stay here as long as they let me."

Cycling City in a Sea of Green

Three decades after Max van de Berg made the bold move of implementing Groningen's Traffic Circulation Plan, and nearly 8,000 kilometers away, another young politician—also early in his career—pushed his hometown along a similarly positive, albeit challenging, path forward. Situated at the southwestern-most point of Canada, Vancouver is similar in size and population to Amsterdam or Rotterdam, with a reputation as haven for people living active lifestyles.

Referred to as a "City in a Sea of Green" in one of its mid-century planning documents, Vancouver, the principal city of the province of British Columbia, sits nestled between the Pacific Ocean and the North Shore Mountains of the coastal range, with access to hiking, paddling, skiing, snowboarding, mountain biking, and any number of other outdoor activities, enjoyed year-round thanks to a temperate rainforest climate. To visitors and residents alike, it is a highly attractive urban playground, which helps to account for its steady population growth as it draws new residents from across Canada and around the world.

But despite Vancouver's reputation for active living, that growth—paired with ever-increasing housing costs—has resulted in an expansion in surrounding suburbs for those in search of more affordable living, and with that an increase in the number of cars entering the city. While Vancouver's traffic woes do not come close to those experienced in other West Coast cities like Seattle, San Francisco, and Los Angeles, residents nonetheless were growing more frustrated with the conditions of their streets and the stress of getting around town.

Enter Gregor Robertson, a local entrepreneur with a genuine desire to improve the quality of life in Vancouver. In 2008, at the age of 44, he successfully won his bid for mayor on the platform of making Vancouver the "World's Greenest City" by 2020—a lofty goal that included drastically increasing the cycling modal share, which at the time sat at a paltry 3.7 percent. To achieve this, Robertson would embark on a path filled with ample conflict and plenty of "bikelash," all in the name of progress.

"Given our compact core city, which more closely resembles European cities than most other North American cities, that combination is an ideal place to take cycling to the next level," Robertson explains, referencing Vancouver's absence of urban freeways, a tighter street grid, mixed-use zoning, and geographic boundaries that limit horizontal growth in every direction. "We wanted to enable many more people to get out of their cars and get active, reducing traffic congestion, and the missing ingredient was the infrastructure to ensure that they felt safe," he explains. Almost from day one, Robertson and his council began work on the first of many new street improvements— physically separated bike lanes on the six-lane Burrard Street Bridge.

A critical link between the city's west side neighborhoods and the downtown peninsula, this bridge had been the site of many tragic collisions between cars and vulnerable road users, and was the focus of countless "Critical Mass" protest bike rides demanding safer streets. "I think people forget now, but there were thousands of people protesting the lack of bike infrastructure prior to 2008," Robertson recalls. "Our first job was to make sure we were addressing those big safety concerns."

But if reallocating one travel lane from cars to bikes to address clear safety concerns seemed like an uncontroversial move, Robertson quickly learned otherwise. From the moment the plan was announced, the blowback began. Media outlets published scathing editorials about how "Mayor Moonbeam" was making it impossible to get anywhere in the city by car, and residents would turn up at council meetings to voice their vehement opposition to the proposed change. Robertson and his council forged ahead, though, opening the unidirectional bike lanes in August of 2009. "A few loud critics can make anything look controversial," he points out. "I recall all the media outlets doing full coverage of the Burrard Bridge opening, big choppers overhead, filming the impending chaos—and it was much ado about nothing. It had zero impact on traffic from day one."

Since then, the bridge has become one of the city's most heavily traveled bike routes, and in the summer of 2017—eight years after the redesign debuted—bicycle traffic hit a total of 9 million unique trips, a fact that has justified further reallocation of space, with a second lane of car traffic removed to create more space for people on foot and bike on either side of the bridge deck. Not bad for a project that many local pundits predicted would mark not just the beginning but also the end of Robertson's political career.

Acknowledging that a single bike route wouldn't solve the city's transportation problems, Robertson spent the next nine years—and two successful re-election campaigns—building an "AAA" ("All Ages and Abilities") network of bike infrastructure across the city, with a heavy focus on physical separation, especially in the downtown peninsula. As Robertson explains, the City of Vancouver's "Transportation 2040" plan is focused on reducing the number of cars on its streets: "We simply can't add more cars into Vancouver, particularly downtown." By building safe, separated bicycle infrastructure on some of their busiest streets, Robertson hopes to entice people out of their cars and onto bikes. The first two major downtown projects—the Dunsmuir and Hornby Streets protected bike lanes—would prove to be a turning point in the discussions about cycling in Vancouver, but not without their own flashpoints.

Figure 3-4: Prior to 2010, Vancouver's Dunsmuir Viaduct was a three-lane traffic sewer. Handing one lane over to bikes has induced a total of 3.7 million unique trips. (Credit: Modacity)

In hindsight, it's clear that Robertson would have benefited from De Rook's advice regarding his approach to the business community, especially during the construction along Hornby and Dunsmuir Streets. The Downtown Vancouver Business Improvement Association (DVBIA), headed by its president and CEO, Charles Gauthier, came out in full force against the improvements, feeling the City was moving too quickly and without sufficient consultation with their members. Instead, the City opted to forge ahead, and the DVBIA took offence. "There's a fine balance," Robertson admits, "between taking action to keep people safe on the streets and ensuring there's appropriate consultation." Still, he doesn't regret the decision. "For me, I'd rather err on the side of saving lives than taking extra months to talk about it."

While the Burrard Street Bridge experienced almost instant success, Dunsmuir and Hornby Streets—critical pieces in creating a grid-like bike-lane network—saw a slower uptake in cycling numbers, which only fueled the controversy. Gauthier infamously stated, "We have to ensure that we're not choking the lifeblood out of the downtown." Many bike advocates recall the iconic image of Mike Brascia, a downtown tailor, standing in the middle of an underutilized Hornby Street bike lane, his arms outstretched, bemoaning the lack of parking for his customers. It may have been a more meaningful statement, however, if he weren't standing next to a half-empty multistory parking garage.

Robertson has since learned his lesson. He now ensures that the Business Improvement Associations are more involved in the conversation from the start: "The BIAs are justifiably concerned about the interests of their business owners, despite data and reports from other cities that bike lanes are good for business." As new sections are added to the network, the proof of their success is becoming more and more apparent, changing the hearts and minds of even their most vocal opponents. "Once the numbers became obvious, they've become big supporters," Robertson declares.

Nowhere is that more obvious than with the aforementioned DVBIA. In the summer of 2015, they launched "Re-Imagine Downtown"—an extensive public-engagement process that asked residents and visitors how they envisioned a more resilient and competitive city center might take shape over the next 25 years. After polling 11,000 people, the results challenged many of the their core assumptions and beliefs, with a clear majority desiring a more walkable, bikeable, people-oriented downtown, and with just 6 percent of respondents saying they wanted more space for cars.

Gauthier and the DVBIA heard their customers loud and clear. And to his immense credit, Gauthier has become one of the city's most vocal proponents of bicycle infrastructure, reversing his organization's position on the protected bike lanes on Dunsmuir and Hornby Streets (he now calls them "the way of the future"), supporting the most recent walking and cycling improvements to the Burrard Street Bridge (a "win–win–win for all users"), championing the arrival of bike-share to Vancouver, and even hosting HUB Cycling's annual "Bike-Friendly Business Awards." In early 2017, the DVBIA cemented this progression with a platinum HUB membership, making a $15,000 annual commitment to the nonprofit advocacy group to invest in initiatives such as "Bike to Work Week" and "Bike to Shop Days."

When asked about how such a dramatic change of heart can influence other business leaders in the city, Robertson says, "I'm hopeful that our successes in some parts of the city make it easier to go forward to building a complete streets network in others. That's what we're all striving for—making our streets vibrant, safe, and engaging, and that means supporting all forms of transportation and ensuring that active transportation is part of the landscape." He is quick to note that, while much of the council's focus has outwardly appeared fixated on cycling, their commitment to the transportation hierarchy matches that of Groningen, putting walking first, cycling second, public transportation third, and then private cars at the bottom of the priority list.

Throughout all of this pushback and opposition, Vancouver has experienced an authentic bike boom, with the modal share increasing by nearly 300 percent. As of May 2016, 10 percent of trips to work were made by bike, one of the highest rates in North America. The most striking changes, however, have been qualitative. Many longtime Vancouverites can recall the days before the bike lanes—with sporty cyclists, predominantly men, on road bikes jostling for space on busy streets where cycling was only for the fit and the brave. Nowadays, the city's seawall, cycle tracks, and neighborhood greenways are awash with residents of all ages and abilities enjoying safe, comfortable bike trips to school, work, shops, and everywhere in between. "We've seen an incredible growth in the number of people riding bikes, especially women, children, and the elderly," Robertson submits. While they didn't specifically predict this shift, women now make up nearly half of all trips made by bicycle.

That's not to say that opposition has completely disappeared. "The media has overinflated how controversial it is," claims Robertson. "The changes have been positive, but there's a perception among car drivers and media that there's a negative impact, which doesn't bear out in the data or research." He is confident that Vancouver has reached a cultural tipping point, with a quiet majority of residents very much in favor of the infrastructure improvements and the positive impact it is having on the health and happiness of people living in and moving around the city.

Today, with few exceptions, it is rare to read anything negative about the building of bike lanes—if anything is written at all—and Vancouver is well on its way to having a complete, citywide AAA network connecting east to west and north to south. When asked whether or not the fight was worth it, Robertson is confident that he's on the correct side of history: "It's the right thing to do. Change is always challenging, particularly when it involves daily commutes, and we've had an aggressive commitment to ensure we make cycling safer in Vancouver. It's great for quality of life—people are getting active and healthier, and our streets are safer and less congested. It's a win–win."

04 ONE SIZE WON'T FIT ALL

*Humans make errors and willingly or unwillingly break rules.
This is a given that cannot be changed. So roads and streets
should be designed in such a way that this natural human
behavior does not lead to crashes and injuries.*

— DUTCH INSTITUTE FOR ROAD SAFETY RESEARCH
Sustainable Safety Principles

Vancouver is just one of countless cities implementing strategic cycling plans, each with the goal of getting more people riding more often. But even with this forward momentum, there persists an erroneous belief that, while the Dutch can provide encouragement, their methods are unrepeatable and results unattainable. Miles of dedicated cycle tracks, bike streets, and off-street bikeways are something that only works for "them" and not "us." However, as Janette Sadik-Khan has implied, even the Netherlands had to start somewhere. So can the country that has spent decades building comfortable cycling infrastructure provide a blueprint for North American cities?

Each year, delegations of engineers, planners, city officials, and general enthusiasts visit cities such as Rotterdam, Groningen, and Amsterdam to experience and perhaps to be inspired by the brilliance of a matured cycling culture that appears to work so effortlessly. Meredith Glaser, a researcher at the University of Amsterdam's Urban Cycling Institute, hosts many of these groups through a partnership with the US-based nonprofit PeopleForBikes, and often surprises them by revealing that many of the Netherlands' successes actually have very little to do with the bicycle.

In 1992, a new approach was adopted by the Dutch national government called *Duurzaam Veilig* ("Sustainable Safety"), a Swedish concept that Dutch road managers happily took and adapted to their own context. "It's more than bike-network design, but rather a broader approach to safe streets," Glaser explains. "Sustainable Safety is about systematic road safety, an approach that looks at the volumes of cars and the speeds at which they travel on any given street, and then offers guidance on the types of infrastructure that should be found on those streets." While the phrase itself can be a bit misleading— Sustainable Safety has nothing to do with environmental sustainability—it is no longer just a European idea, having been adapted from its Swedish origins into the "Vision Zero" policy now gaining traction across North America.

"Large differences in speed and mass of different road users in the same space must be eliminated as much as possible. Road users can best be forced to travel at lower speeds by road design," state the Sustainable Safety principles succinctly. This systematic, safe-streets approach established three main road categories, as well as their corresponding bicycle infrastructure, all of which is prescribed in the Dutch *Design Manual for Bicycle Traffic* (generally known as the CROW Manual, from the acronym of the *Centrum voor Regelgeving en Onderzoek in de Wegenbouw*—the "Center for Regulation and Research in Road Construction and Traffic Engineering").

- *Stroomwegen* ("Flow/Through Roads") are designed to move a large volume of cars at speeds over 100 km/h (60 mph). North Americans would define these as highways and interstates. On such roads, physical separation of motorized traffic and bicycles is mandatory, often achieved through a nearby separated cycling path, like the new cycle superhighways being built across the country, or a parallel road where conditions are vastly safer.

- *Gebiedsontsluitingswegen* ("Distributor Roads") are essentially arterial roads; speeds here range between 50 km/h (30 mph) and 70 km/h (40 mph). They are designed for flow but include exchanges at intersections, whether junctions or roundabouts. Separation is still mandatory between fast and slow users. This can be achieved through three types of cycle tracks. Segregated cycle tracks are physically separated from the road space through the use of a wide median or grass. Protected cycle tracks are adjacent to the road space but provide protection via the use of parked cars, cement barriers, planters, bollards, or a painted buffer. Raised cycle tracks are adjacent to the road, but elevated to indicate the space is dedicated to bicycles.

- *Erftoegangswegen* ("Access Roads") are neighborhood roads where modes can mix thanks to reduced speeds. On rural or regional access roads, this can be up to 60 km/h (35 mph), and ideally there is physical separation between modes. However, in dense urban areas the speeds cannot exceed 30 km/h (20 mph), and signage and road surface treatments are used to clearly identify it as a shared space. The one exception is a *woonerf* ("living street"), where speeds are limited to 15 km/h (10 mph), and pedestrians rule the road. Considered to be extensions of the living room, *woonerfs* are outdoor spaces for play and socialization, where parking is limited and driving is made inconvenient and thus is avoided by most except people who live locally.

Glaser is quick to point out that these delineations between road and infrastructure types are just one part of the equation: "The basic tenets of bike network design are that it must be continuous, recognizable, safe, and intuitive for all users." Cycling infrastructure of any kind is of little use to anyone if it doesn't connect them to where they want to go, which is why looking at the cycling maps of any Dutch city will show a well-connected web of bike routes that take travelers directly to their destination without sacrificing comfort or convenience.

That continuity goes hand in hand with being recognizable, and is achieved in several ways. Of course, the most recognizable treatment for both locals and anyone who has visited the Netherlands is the ubiquitous red pavement—a 3-centimeter- (1-inch-) thick top layer of special dyed-red asphalt that is used for all separated cycle tracks, most bike lanes, and any *fietsstraat* ("bicycle street"). For neighborhood streets, cities often use paving

Figure 4-1: The CROW Manual mandates separated cycle tracks on all "Distributor Roads," like this one on Amsterdam's Jan Pieter Heijestraat. (Credit: Modacity)

stones, usually a similar red to that of the cycle tracks, which not only identify a space as shared, but also serve to slow cars.

"If you travel from an arterial to a residential street, there's a difference in materials, elevation, and cues in the environment used to slow cars down," Glaser explains. "For example, a car driver would cross onto what I would call a 'welcome mat,' an elevated area at the same level as the bicycle and pedestrian pathway. This creates a shared-space situation where a driver has to traverse over the foot- and cycle-path and back down to street level, where the textures again would change. Drivers immediately understand they are in a different space and need to watch out."

Glaser points out that the treatment of cyclists and pedestrians is glaringly different in North America. Originally from the San Francisco Bay Area, she recalls a childhood spent stepping down into the dangerous "driving zone" to cross a street, and she loves that her daughter, by contrast, is growing up in a place where drivers have to slow to a crawl and move up into the walking and cycling space—treated as a trespasser—before going back down again. "It really levels the playing field. All types of road users are on this same space and you have to negotiate with each other," she points out. "That sense of entitlement is decreased—if not eliminated entirely—and you have to really interact with everyone in these spaces."

A clear, continuous network is important in order to permit safe travel throughout a city, but Glaser argues that making it intuitive supersedes any other quality. "It's an important component to the Dutch approach," she says, "because context is paramount for Dutch bike network design. There is no copy-paste solution, there's no prescription for each street. Each one really has its own way of fitting within the network." The treatment of a street or intersection, and how it connects to others in a complete network, is selected based on the travel patterns of its users. This eliminates the need for indicators or signage to tell users how to behave; they already know instinctively.

This idea seems counterintuitive in an age where bicycle infrastructure is being prescribed as the "cure-all" for getting more people cycling elsewhere in the world. As Glaser points out, elements such as land use and local context play a huge role in how a street will be treated: "When it comes down to it, the street itself will dictate what type of solution will be employed there." She uses the example of the street on which she lives, which is home to the local elementary school. Sections of the adjacent street are restricted solely to bike and scooter/moped access, allowing more space for bicycle parking and even a small playground. No special car parking is available, which limits the number of parents who drive their children to and from school. Adapting streets in this way—along with more efficient land-use planning—is one of the reasons why the number of children driven to school in the Netherlands is dramatically lower than elsewhere; whereas 86 percent of Dutch kids walk or bike to school, only 11 percent do so in the United States. Here again, though, Glaser is clear that solutions like the one working in her neighborhood are not always applied to the entire street: "Context is used where it's needed."

All of these tenets—continuity, recognition, safety, and intuitiveness—combine to establish one guiding principle that Glaser says is key to success: "It's really about intensive traffic-calming, moving as many people through the street as possible, and that's what the Dutch approach does." Elements like wider sidewalks, slower speeds, reduced and expensive parking, and rerouting cars—when combined with a complete bicycle network—get more people traveling through the city because they use the land in a way that brings destinations closer together. From home, to school, to work, to the grocer and back, all in the most suitable and efficient way possible.

From across the Atlantic, the highly evolved bicycle networks and long-established cycling culture enjoyed in the Netherlands may look intimidating to planners just breaking ground on their own designs, but, as Glaser notes, what may look like a "finished product" never has been, nor ever will be. "The streets here have also gone through several different renditions throughout the years, so they're not something that's a fixed solution either." She drives this fact home as she takes delegations from around the globe through her adopted home of Amsterdam, showing off some of its historical transformations—like the successful freeway fight on Jodenbreestraat—and the new experiments that she and her Urban Cycling Institute colleagues are researching across town, with the hope of sharing inspiring ideas that visitors can take back to their own cities. "The simple act of being able to imagine oneself on a bike is much more complex than it seems," reflects Glaser. "So coming to a place to experience it firsthand seems to have an effect on that ability to imagine and also the ability to talk about mobility in a different way. But, in the end, it's still not about bikes and even bike lanes or putting more bikes on the streets. It's about safety. It's about comfort. It's about having strong cities that are economically viable and wonderful places to be."

Translating Dutch Ideas for the World

Glaser will admit that translating the complex concept of increasing resiliency and economic viability through street design is a difficult task, so just how can the Dutch clearly communicate their successful tactics to a broader audience, without elements getting lost in translation? Mirjam Borsboom, director of the Dutch Cycling Embassy and founder of Movida Transport Solutions, is pragmatic in her methodology: "Every city has its own characteristics, inhabitants, habits and cultures, so there is one way for every city—you just need to find out what that is."

Located in Delft, the Dutch Cycling Embassy is a nonprofit established in 2011 with one clear mission: "Cycling for Everyone." They mean that in the broadest sense. "It's providing the opportunity for everyone at least willing to use a bicycle to have access to one in every country," Borsboom says. "As soon as everyone has the choice to use a bicycle to get where they want to go, our mission will be accomplished."

Through public–private partnerships, Borsboom and her small but influential team coordinate a network of Dutch private partners, NGOs, and universities, as well as anyone consulting on cycling in the Netherlands. The Dutch Cycling Embassy connects them to organizations, governments, and businesses from around the world interested in gaining their perspective. "We try to help as much as we can, providing information on anything from education, children, infrastructure, and social inclusion to technical designs. It's super-diverse, and every day is different," she says enthusiastically.

The Dutch Cycling Embassy handles all kinds of requests. They share information, connect delegations from other countries with experts, speak at conferences, and run "ThinkBike" workshops and seminars—essentially anything an organization can dream up to learn more about the Dutch experience. Oftentimes, this includes traveling to other countries to help them develop cycling programs. Since 2011, they have worked with 39 North American organizations and many more globally, each with varying needs and requests. For those that require travel, they coordinate bringing relevant partners along, helping to fill the gap depending on which questions may come up.

Interestingly, though, no matter where they visit, their approach is always centered on the same thing that it is back home: context. "I always like to respond to people who say 'This isn't the Netherlands'—because we hear it a lot—that cities in the Netherlands are different, too," Borsboom explains.

"Rotterdam and Amsterdam are two very different cities, and smaller cities also have their own culture and habits. There's always a way for every city, you just need to figure out which way that is." During their visits, they recommend a starting point, always recognizing what works for one community may not for another, but setting that foundation allows them to identify what challenges they are able to address and how. Borsboom does note that a particular challenge when translating ideas to North American cities is one of perspective: "It's always fun to hear things like, 'Oh, there's not enough space!' But really, you have so much space, you just can't see it."

Figure 4-2: As extensions of the living room, *woonerfs* ("living streets") are traffic calmed to 15 km/h, such as this one on Utrecht's Kapelstraat. (Credit: Modacity)

When working on infrastructure plans, Borsboom generally recommends three things to begin with: roundabouts, a network approach, and a "back streets" principle. The latter refers to shifting bike routes off main arterials with heavy traffic volumes and onto adjacent side streets, increasing the comfort of cyclists and limiting the amount of investment required for separated infrastructure. Once again, just as on Dutch roads, the ideas of traffic-calming, safety, continuity, and intuition are the benchmarks of any proposed changes. She has noticed that a number of cities are now removing stop signs in favor of roundabouts, a treatment that serves to slow automobile traffic without restricting their flow—a bit of a win–win. In Vancouver, this is a common element seen along their bicycle boulevards—the North American version of a *fietsstraat*—and, in Borsboom's opinion, a definite step forward.

Connection, however, really is the critical ingredient, "I think the network approach is very important for cycling infrastructure," she insists. "It's better to have a bit of connection—one or two loops or interchanges but still connected—compared to all these cities that skip things like intersections, which are the hardest part for people on bikes."

Everyone involved with the Dutch Cycling Embassy recognizes that they have an obligation to carefully consider the path forward for cycling. Considered experts in most cycling circles, Borsboom, the Embassy team, and their Dutch partners are positioned to continue having the hard conversations with other cities, in order to open their eyes to what is possible, and challenge their preconceived ideas about what isn't. "I think it's important to have organizations pushing the higher levels to make things better for cycling," states Borsboom. Any city looking at boosting cycling numbers tends to focus heavily on building the "hardware"—safe and reliable cycling infrastructure designed to form a complete network. But Borsboom also emphasizes the importance of paying attention to the "software" component: encouraging behavior change and the mindset of the community. Not everyone rides a bicycle or even wants to, and organizations need to take that into account in their planning.

With that in mind, Borsboom and her team tend to look at the context of the places they are working with and the particular challenges they are experiencing in getting people to adopt cycling as a mode of transportation, and they adapt the conversation to one that is less about prescribing the solution than one where they are collaborating on something that will work best for the given situation. "You need to find the right argument for the person that's sitting on the other side of the table," she says.

Of all the work they've done over the years, Borsboom views their cooperation with the US Federal Highway Administration in 2015, and subsequent projects with the cities of Milwaukee, Detroit, and Washington, DC, as especially important. "It's quite hard in every country to get everybody— all these different parties and opinions—together and to send them on this joint mission to help," she admits. "They all have their own perspectives, goals, and expectations. And to have aligned all those expectations while also reaching the consensus they did within a week is quite an achievement, not only for them but also for us. We really learned from the experience, and the professional level we reached is now used to improve on other work we do."

Borsboom sees a shift happening on a much more global scale, especially in North America and New Zealand, which she thinks are leading the charge in the new wave of bicycle adoption. She notes that many of the current fights occurring outside the Netherlands are no different from the ones that happened in Dutch cities in the 1970s and '80s. It's quite easy to forget that it was just a couple of generations ago that Amsterdam was widening roads, Utrecht was burying their canal beneath a motorway, and Rotterdam's city center was a desolate place to be, all for the sake of making driving easier. Everything is dependent on examining the local context, behaviors, and habits, developing the basics first and then getting more creative.

When asked about the Dutch Cycling Embassy's influence elsewhere, Borsboom is confident they are having a positive impact. "It's so great to see the results of your efforts, and to be at the beginning of the tipping point in North America," she reflects. "I think it's really exciting. Every time I visit I see so much changing, and I'd like to believe we are at a changing point. It may be naïve, but I like to think positively, and I truly believe that we are at a unique moment in history."

Capturing Car Trips in the Heart of Texas

A full 40 years after the Dutch experienced their own cultural tipping point, similar signs are being spotted on this side of the Atlantic, and in the unlikeliest of places. Places such as the Texas capital of Austin, which—despite considering itself a progressive oasis in a staunchly conservative desert—bears a striking physical resemblance to its car-dependent counterparts in Houston, San Antonio, Dallas, Fort Worth, and El Paso. Decades of unrestricted, auto-centric planning and policy have created vast, sprawling metropolises, which are among the highest in the country when ranked by population numbers and total area, and the lowest when it comes to population density.

Residents of these regions have virtually no choice when it comes to getting around—a condition aptly described as "transport poverty"—worsening the ever-familiar concerns of affordability, congestion, and social equity. The bicycle, seen as a tool for recreation but not transportation, has been reduced to the margins, making up just 1 percent of trips. In Austin, though, a consensus led by the City's Active Transportation Division has emerged that attracting new people to cycling can address a great number of the city's most pressing issues. In the last few years, the groundwork has been laid for an ambitious AAA bike network, the vision for which came through strategic partnerships with PeopleForBikes and the Dutch Cycling Embassy.

"We'd been following the development of protected infrastructure since stumbling across [City of Portland bicycle coordinator] Roger Geller's 2006 paper on the 'interested, but concerned' cyclist in 2010," reveals City of Austin transportation planner and street designer Nathan Wilkes. "We were also watching what Janette Sadik-Khan was doing in New York." The subsequent release of the NACTO *Urban Street Design Guide* helped codify many of these foreign concepts that were then outside the realm of existing policy, and Wilkes began developing the notion of an AAA network of cycle routes, which would form the basis of a pitch to PeopleForBikes' Green Lane Project.

"Working with PeopleForBikes came a little out of the blue, but ended up being a pretty transformative process," recalls Lauren Dierenfield, the City's Active Transportation Division manager. In 2011, the Boulder-based

PeopleForBikes—an industry coalition of American bicycle manufacturers and retailers—was seeking partner cities for its Green Lane Project, a five-year initiative to accelerate the spread of protected cycling facilities. One of Austin's more informed, passionate, and savvy advocates suggested that City staff should look into applying, and the rest was history. "It set the stage for an overhaul of our Bicycle Master Plan, for all-ages-and-abilities cycling infrastructure," recalls Dierenfield enthusiastically. "The process was very much inspired by the Dutch, but reinterpreted for a retrofit environment."

Recognizing that cultural change must precede structural change, the Green Lane Project intelligently initiated a pair of tactical exercises, aimed at decision makers and the general electorate. The first was financing a delegation of four, including Austin's city manager, bicycle program manager, public works director, and a council member, to join Meredith Glaser's study tour of the Netherlands in 2011. A second delegation, including the city's head traffic engineer, was sent in 2012.

PeopleForBikes also connected Dierenfield's department with the Dutch Cycling Embassy, which traveled to Texas to conduct a ThinkBike Workshop in October 2012. The two-day program assembled politicians, planners, advocates, engineers, and entrepreneurs to engage in the planning process and discuss how Dutch principles could be applied to a local context. "They were mind-blowing," raves Dierenfield. "They changed our entire thinking about bicycle planning and design."

"There were four big 'aha' moments from the ThinkBike event," explains Wilkes. "The first was, we needed to get used to spending more money on bikes. The second was, we needed to focus investment on areas where we could capture short trips. The third was, we needed to use bicycling to feed transit. And the last was, we couldn't do bike-network planning without also planning for all modes." Each of these points was underlined by an understanding that any successful network must reflect CROW principles of cohesion, directness, safety, attractiveness, and comfort.

The ThinkBike Workshop also featured the unveiling of the "MOVE Meter," a groundbreaking web-based traffic-modeling tool, developed by the Dutch firm MOVE Mobility, that maps the frequency and distance of automobile trips in a given setting. When fed with the region's travel-demand data—making Austin the first American city to utilize this asset—it created a heat map of car trips of less than five kilometers (three miles), the low-hanging fruit of active-transportation planners everywhere. "During the workshop, we were able to zoom into certain busy intersections and note that over half of those cars were traveling under three miles," remembers Wilkes.

By overlaying this heat map onto the proposed bike network, and adjusting the latter to affect the biggest impact, the Dutch Cycling Embassy were able to advise how many automobile trips could be replaced by the bicycle—if conditions were made comfortable and convenient enough. "They suggested that for car trips less than three miles, we could capture 15 percent," recounts Wilkes. "And later we added 7 percent of trips between three and nine miles, based on their actual data." He claims those numbers are somewhat conservative, set at roughly a third of the Dutch national average, which would easily be achieved with a fully realized bike network, even in an auto-oriented American city. While cautious in their predictions, the Austin planning team realized that capturing short trips at these levels would result in a significant reduction in driving times, especially in the congested area where many of these trips are located: the city center.

Needless to say, the knowledge and ideas collected in that short period of time required a shift in strategy, officially summarized in the City of Austin's 2014 Bicycle Master Plan, principally authored by Wilkes—with the help of a $20,000 PeopleForBikes grant—and adopted by the Austin City Council in November 2014. "Our 2009 Bike Plan was written in service to people who are bicyclists," he explains. "The way we flipped it around in 2014 was to use bicycling as a tool that would serve the highest goals of our city articulated in the 'Imagine Austin Comprehensive Plan.' We documented a strong case of community benefit, for a much wider-scale investment in a network that would make bicycling a safe choice for everybody for almost every trip." The visionary new plan spelled out a $150-million, 600-kilometer (373-mile) network roughly divided into thirds: one-third consisting of off-street trails, one-third consisting of on-street protected or higher-quality buffered bike lanes, and one-third consisting of quiet neighborhood streets that provide connections between the other two assets.

Figure 4-3: The Dutch-inspired 3rd Street cycle track is the last piece of a fully connected, eight-kilometer (five-mile) sequence of AAA routes across downtown Austin.
(Credit: City of Austin)

Faced with finding a way to pay for these critical upgrades, along with
other mobility needs, the City of Austin placed a $720-million mobility bond
on the November 2016 ballot, $46 million of which would be used directly on
bike projects, with a number of other portions of the bond also significantly
supporting bicycle infrastructure. While Dierenfield and her team were not
allowed to participate directly in the election campaign, the benefits were
well documented in the adopted plan, the news of which advocates were
more than happy to spread far and wide.

To complement their efforts, Austin mayor Steve Adler declared 2016
the "Year of Mobility," and in the spring, he participated in a study tour of
the Netherlands, Denmark, and Norway. Funded by the US Department of
Transportation's "Smart City Challenge," Adler was joined by Austin's transportation director Robert Spillar and US transportation secretary Anthony
Foxx, who were photographed pedaling e-bikes on the streets of Amsterdam. "Most people aren't going to get out of their cars anytime soon in Austin," Adler reflected in a blog post. "But no significant number will ever be

ready to get out of their cars unless or until there are alternatives. We have work to do in Austin, and I was glad to see that it can work in Amsterdam."

Clearly, Austin's leaders had done an effective job in communicating exactly what was at stake, and the bond passed with an impressive 59 percent of the vote. "It exceeded anybody's expectations," admits Wilkes, whose department now has five years in which to spend an amount of money that would have been a pipe dream a few years prior.

Two months after the proposition's passage, PeopleForBikes announced that Austin was one of 10 US cities selected for the "Big Jump Project," a new scheme focused on developing networks that triple the number of people biking there by 2020. "We feel very fortunate to be part of this 'Big Jump' cohort of cities," says Dierenfield. "With this new opportunity, we see huge value in continuing to use the study-tour tool to allow that same level of discovery, understanding, and appreciation of how street design can achieve common goals of affordability, mobility, and quality of life."

One of the first steps was to send a member of their team, transportation planner and street designer Alison Mills, to the Velo-City Global Cycling Summit in Nijmegen, the Netherlands, in June 2017. "They do have this really impressive separated infrastructure, but to me, the importance of safe, well-designed shared street settings became apparent," Mills says of her Dutch experience. "Everything they do there is not completely separated. A really important part of a network is managing to get those pieces as well, that connect to the separated infrastructure." According to Dierenfield, Mills' week in the Netherlands will bring a new perspective to a fast-tracked process: "She'll be leading a team of designers shortly, as we graduate into some new models for project development and delivery. Having that understanding under her belt provides much more value to the team."

And so the coming years promise to be eventful indeed for bicycling in Austin, and the City's staff know that they will still be able to discuss future concerns with the Dutch Cycling Embassy, despite their contractual relationship ending with the 2012 ThinkBike Workshop. "It's always a pleasure to get their insights and reactions to how we're approaching our work," enthuses Wilkes. "It feels like talking to kindred spirits in the future. In many ways, they've been through everything that we've been through. They've been doing it for decades. They've made all the mistakes that we're making. So we just need to do the work, and we'll see where we are in 50 years."

Cycle Superhighways That Fight Congestion

Having mastered the art of converting short trips by car to the more scale-appropriate bicycle, some Dutch jurisdictions are now looking further afield, hoping to capture longer, intercity car trips using a variety of innovative solutions. And while the Netherlands is already crisscrossed with countless rural cycling routes, many of these paths are narrow (at least by Dutch standards), meandering, and riddled with stoppages, making them less desirable choices for commuting outside city limits.

Addressing this challenge head-on is the region of the twin cities of Arn-hem and Nijmegen—located in the province of Gelderland—a collection of 20 different municipalities situated on the eastern border with Germany. By applying "big picture" thinking, as well as a level of funding, planning, and cooperation not typically seen on Dutch cycling projects, they are in the process of developing a network of nine *snelfietsroutes* ("fast cycling routes") that connect their major residential, employment, educational, and commer-cials nodes. These inspiring and trailblazing projects have put the region on the map, giving its planners a competitive edge when to comes to dealing with growth, traffic, and new opportunities to help their 740,000 residents get to work, school, the shop, and everywhere in between. According to Sjors van Duren, cycling consultant at engineering firm Royal HaskoningDHV, and the former Cycling Highway Network project leader for the Province of Gelderland: "The first one, between Arnhem and Nijmegen, was built because, back in 2008, the local chapter of the *Fietsersbond* [Cyclists' Union] went to the vice-mayors and aldermen and said, 'We need a better cycling connection between the cities.'"

Because the project involved four municipalities, those local governments didn't know how to deal with it and so offloaded it onto the regional agenda, fully expecting it to get shelved. But that quickly changed when the national government passed a budgetary amendment to invest more in cycling infra-structure, suddenly earmarking substantial funding for the region. "At a meeting, it was agreed that in addition to €5 million [$6.2 million USD] from the national government, the province would pay €5 million, and the region €3 million [$3.7 million USD]," recalls Van Duren. "We started developing the project, and we got commitments from the municipalities for a total budget of €17 million [$21 million USD]."

Having ditched the decades-old idea that cycling is simply a local issue, Van Duren and his team got to work. They defined a network of links between the places that people lived and where they worked, of distances up to 15 kilometers (9.3 miles), and identified a number of key policy goals. "One of them was reducing car dependency, and seeing if we can provide drivers alternatives to sitting in a traffic jam," he explains. "We saw the connection between accessibility to our main nodes—such as the university and the city center—and the availability of cycling. So it was really a congestion-based approach."

According to Van Duren, one of the secrets of their success was giving the local governments the largest share of ownership, despite their supplying the smallest share of financing. "The municipalities were responsible for tendering the infrastructure, for building the infrastructure, and doing the engagement process themselves," he clarifies. "We would facilitate with studies and support. But it never felt to the municipalities as a top-down project, so they felt like a co-owner of it."

The first such cycle superhighway in the country—named the Rijn-Waalpad ("Rhine–Waal Path") after the two rivers that shape the region's landscape—opened in July 2015, connecting its two largest cities: Arnhem (population: 150,000) and Nijmegen (170,000). It enables the user to ride 16 kilometers (just under 10 miles) in under 45 minutes, without having to stop even once.

Not entirely a new cycle path, the RijnWaalpad pieced together a few existing roads—which were transformed into *fietsstraten*—new stretches of cycle path, and some tunnels and bridges. The overall quality was a significant improvement over the existing, but less direct and desirable, 2.5-meter- (8-foot-) wide, 19 kilometer- (just under 12 mile-) long route. The path was widened to 4 meters (13 feet), with smooth red asphalt, a few shortcuts were added, and several intersections were redesigned to give priority to the bicycle. "It was already safe. Now it was comfortable and convenient," explains Van Duren. "Besides going quick, cyclists also want an attractive and easy-to-navigate route."

As they continued to put other pieces of the planned network into place, Van Duren and his colleagues had to get creative in chasing funding. "A cycle superhighway is nothing more than a concept, consisting of 10 or 20 interlocking projects," he concedes. Not likely to have another €17 million ($21 million USD) fall into their laps, they were forced to identify, assess, and then pursue funding for these individual schemes; a great deal of the money was secured by making the economic case to the general public.

Figure 4-4: As the nation's first cycle superhighway, the RijnWaalpad ("Rhine–Waal Path") allows cyclists to travel 16 kilometers in under 45 minutes without stopping once. (Credit: Modacity)

"We did predictions about how these routes would impact congestion, and quite a bit of funding became available because we were providing alternative modes to travel to and from the city," Van Duren points out. Traffic modeling and cost–benefit analyses became transformative tools in securing financing partners. Van Duren recalls one specific instance where a bicycle tunnel was financed by the road department: "It was near a major intersection, and we said, 'If we build this tunnel, we can remove cyclists from the traffic light, and the phasing will be 30 seconds shorter.'" That junction moved 30,000 cars per day, saving drivers a combined 15,000 minutes in travel time. "Those travel time savings are worth so much, so the tunnel was worth building from a car driver's perspective," asserts Van Duren.

This reinforces the powerful idea that cycle-friendly street improvements can be win–win scenarios for all modes of transportation. "That's the whole idea behind the concept of the cycle superhighway—that you improve conditions for cyclists in order to also improve conditions for the drivers that stay on the road," states Van Duren. "So you provide more alternatives, and you make it more attractive. We're pulling people towards the cycle highway, not pushing them out of their cars."

In the case of the RijnWaalpad, the province found itself in an enviable position as they neared completion: they had approximately €1 million ($1.24 million USD) to allocate to innovation. "We had €17 million in funding, but €16 million in infrastructure investments," recalls Van Duren. "So we decided to invest the remaining €1 million in making the route more attractive, and making sure more people know about it. After all, the stated goal of the project is for people to change their behavior and start using the route." So they went about increasing the impact of their investment, devoting just 6 percent of the budget to an exciting branding and marketing campaign.

A region-wide public contest led to the naming of the route, as well as adopting a logo resembling three rivets of a bike chain. This motif was repeated in a custom-designed and -built light installation that stretches the length of the *snelfietsroute*, colored green when cycling northbound to Arnhem, and purple when heading south to Nijmegen. "They were, of course, intended to light the cycle superhighway," admits Van Duren. "But because it is alongside the railway tracks and motorway between Arnhem and

Nijmegen, they make people aware of the project." That proximity isn't an accident, and serves as a constant, glowing advertisement to a captive audience stuck inside a train or in their automobiles. "That's the first step to change, knowing there's an alternative." It worked. In the neighborhoods surrounding the cycle superhighways, surveys showed that 95 percent of residents were aware of the route and where it was located.

In addition to the fixtures, the province also experimented with game-ification techniques, developing an app that allows the user to play with the colors inside one of the underpasses. Riding the route regularly unlocks new colors in the tunnel's lighting system, encouraging its use, and giving people a sense of pride and ownership in the RijnWaalpad.

Finally, the remainder of this budget was spent reaching out directly to citizens who frequently commute between Arnhem and Nijmegen by automobile. "We said to them 'go ride two in five,'" remembers Van Duren. "From the five days you travel to work each week, try riding your bike one or two of those days. We wanted to convince them there's an alternative, and make them aware of their options."

These investments appear to be paying off, with the busiest segments of the RijnWaalpad seeing upwards of 6,000 cyclists per day, and the project receiving international plaudits as a model to be replicated elsewhere. But most importantly, the route is having a meaningful impact on the behavior of the region's residents.

In late 2015, Van Duren and his team completed a large survey of current RijnWaalpad users, who overwhelmingly noted an improvement in quality, directness, smoothness, signage, and travel times over the previous conditions. Most impressively, one-third of the users were new cyclists, and 20 percent had bought an e-bike because of the RijnWaalpad. "That was really remarkable," notes Van Duren. "I think the combination of the e-bike and the cycle superhighway, it really amplifies the positive effects of the e-bike, which are higher average speeds with less effort."

"It's about setting the right conditions for new cyclists, and that's the group of people that are changing from the car to the bicycle," explains Van Duren. "Because they are buying an e-bike, and they are doing a five- to ten-kilometer [three- to six-mile] commute to work. It's that length of commute that causes the biggest traffic problems, because it's too short for the train, and it's too long for the bus or bicycle. And really, on that level, the cycle superhighway and the e-bike form the perfect combination."

This provides an effective, real-life anecdote to back up Kevin Mayne's insistence that the places with the best bike infrastructure are the ones that sell the most pedelecs, and the global e-bike market won't fulfill its potential without great places to ride. Concludes Van Duren: "Even without the e-bike, the concept of the cycle superhighway can be a game-changer. But with the e-bike it makes it even stronger."

05   DEMAND MORE

Up to here the old city pattern disappeared.
Urban renewal began in this neighborhood.
In commemoration, this memorial set in 1986.

— JODENBREESTRAAT MONUMENT
Amsterdam

Amsterdam is a city filled with monuments, commemorating everything from beloved royalty to forgotten war heroes, but few are as overlooked as the nondescript stone turtle on Jodenbreestraat ("Jewish Broad Street") in the city's historic Jewish Quarter. Nestled between two bustling cycle tracks, and sitting on a stone pedestal that bears a short poem by writer Jacob Israël de Haan, it has come to represent the slow, deliberate pace of a city that consistently chooses the bicycle above all modes of transportation, making up a staggering 70 percent of traffic (including pedestrians!) in the center on a given day. More importantly, this memorial embodies the rejection of a different type of built environment, one that would have looked and felt very different today. While many assume that Amsterdam's status as a world-class cycling city was a given, it quietly reminds passers-by how hard the regular citizens had to fight for that status, and how razor-thin the margins of success were.

"Before the Second World War, Amsterdam was a city where the streets were public spaces," says Cornelia Dinca, graduate of the University of Amsterdam's Urban Planning program and founder of the consultancy group Sustainable Amsterdam. "They were not only for movement, but places for interaction and exchange. There was a lot of buying and selling, and exchange of goods; and because people were living in such small apartments, there was an overflow of activity and street life into the public realm."

Life was highly localized, with neighborhoods centered on the local church, market, and school. "The city was smaller and destinations were closer together, so people were moving less," claims Majorlein de Lange, an Amsterdam-based sustainable mobility and road-safety consultant. "Most movement was done by foot, bike, and public transport. With about ten cars per thousand inhabitants, there were many fewer cars than today, and a lot less space that was dedicated to them."

After the bombing of Rotterdam and a bleak, five-year German occupation during which the streets, buildings, and plazas throughout the Netherlands were neglected, Amsterdammers were desperate to revitalize their city. And modernist planners were more than happy to oblige, selling them on a model of growth that provided more light, air, and space. Plans were drafted to separate the functions of the city, pushing housing to the outskirts, from which residents would commute into the center, now solely dedicated to the economy. With no room for nostalgia, such plans slated much of the old city fabric for demolition so that large, mono-functional buildings for banks, institutions, and services could be built, along with the roads and parking garages that would support the growing volume of car traffic moving in and out of the suburbs.

Crucially, this scheme also involved a rethinking of the street as a shared amenity. "The idea was to move the public-space function into a park, or somewhere else," argues Dinca. "That's the fundamental difference between the pre- and postwar mentality. The postwar city was about the street acting as a channel of movement for cars." That seismic shift in attitude—along with a rise in distances traveled—had an obvious effect, and the growth in automobile traffic was much swifter than anticipated: "The car traffic overran the city," explains de Lange. "But in the existing, prewar city, streets were narrow, and there was no space for them. There you could see a clash between cars and cyclists, traffic jams, and problems with parking."

Proposals to address the clogged streets were myriad. Perhaps the most egregious was a 1954 scheme by Police Commissioner Hendrik Kaasjager,

Figure 5-1: Jodenbreestraat's stone turtle reminds passers-by how hard the citizens had to fight for Amsterdam's status as a world-class cycling city. (Credit: Modacity)

who suggested filling in most of the canals to build a series of ring roads and parking structures. "I stand behind Kaasjager: fill in nine-tenths of the canals as soon as possible," wrote businessman Pieter Van Dijk in *Het Vrije Volk* ("The Free People"). "Construct wide ring-boulevards. Our children and grandchildren will not care about those canals. And you can always leave a few." While a similar plan was started—and eventually abandoned—in nearby Utrecht, Amsterdammers were not the least bit interested in losing one of their most treasured assets. "That plan was ridiculed by most people in the city," says de Lange. "That ended the discussion of filling in the canals for roads."

Another such proposition was a 1961 study written by young American traffic engineer David Jokinen, working in the Netherlands as a well-funded lobbyist for Stichting Weg ("Road Foundation"), a pro-business pressure group. Jokinen's report, entitled *Geef de Stad een Kans* ("Give the City a Chance"), envisioned a motoring metropolis in the spirit of Robert Moses, who—at the time—was busy devastating New York City neighborhoods, waterfronts, and shopping districts with his own grandiose network of freeways. Jokinen proposed American-style expressways that would segment Amsterdam in virtually every direction, along with large-scale parking garages near common destinations. "What it really meant was 'give the city a chance for the car,'" submits Dinca. "Having living and working together was seen as incompatible."

In the 10-year period between 1960 and 1970, the number of cars in the city quadrupled, spurring outrage and discontent among a small but ultimately influential subculture of society. "The asphalt terror of the motorized bourgeoisie has lasted long enough," declares the first line of the manifesto distributed on the streets of Amsterdam via a stenciled leaflet dated May 25, 1965, by the young activists and provocateurs who called themselves the Provos. And with that act, a political movement was born, demanding that the city center be closed to all motor vehicle traffic and instead be served by a fleet of 20,000 white bicycles, free for everybody to use. "The bicycle is something but almost nothing," it concluded, poetically capturing how such a simple machine could solve so many complex problems.

In 1966, at the peak of their powers, the Provos managed to secure a single seat on the city council, but they didn't directly affect any decision-making during that period. However, their regular "happenings"—on-street gatherings intended to disrupt the flow of traffic—planted a seed of dissent that would soon grow into the mainstream. "They were really among the first ones to put their finger on the negative impacts the car was having on the city, on public space, and on livability," recalls Dinca.

And then, in 1972, in what many consider a major turning point, the Amsterdam city council considered a draft *Verkeersplan* ("Traffic Plan") that adopted some of Jokinen's ideas and was fixated entirely on moving people via cars and trains. The 1972 Traffic Plan implied that these two modes of transportation would eventually "win out" for road space, and it failed to mention cycling once—an anachronistic mode seemingly in decline. "Because you're putting everyone further away from where they live," explains Dinca, "the distances that were being traveled increased significantly. And the only way for that to be acceptable is if you can travel these distances at a high speed."

Part of the draft plan involved constructing a four-lane, at-grade motor-way on top of an underground metro line; together they would connect com-muters living in Amsterdam's eastern suburbs with the city center. Much of the corridor in between would be unceremoniously razed to the ground, including the historic neighborhood surrounding Jodenbreestraat. Its Jewish inhabitants had largely abandoned this area after the traumas of the Second World War, and squatters, artists, and poets—many of whom were members of the Provos—then populated it. "The idea was to give the street level to cars, and to put people underground in the metro system, and they would all travel at high speeds," says Dinca. "This would be the city of the future."

The blowback was swift and monumental, leading to the founding of dozens of grassroots activist groups, the largest and most persuasive being Stop de Kindermoord ("Stop Child Murder"), formed in response to an eponymously titled, full-page editorial in *De Tijd* ("The Times") by jour-nalist Vic Langenhoff. Langenhoff—grieving the death of his six-year-old daughter, killed while cycling to school one morning—was understandably enraged at the 150-guilder ($50 USD) fine imposed on the driver, as well as a flawed street design that prioritized speed over human life.

His scathing editorial, which claimed that "This country chooses one kilo-meter of motorway over 100 kilometers of safe cycle paths," struck a nerve with parents across the Netherlands, leading to the creation of a nationwide road-safety pressure group spearheaded by Maartje van Putten, a 23-year-old new mother. Their stated goal was "to break through the apathy with which the Dutch people accept the daily current of children in traffic." At that time, motorists in the Netherlands were killing upwards of 3,000 people, 450 of whom were children, each and every year.

Other citizen-led collectives were formed, many representing a spe-cific interest or geographic area, including De Lastige Amsterdammer

("The Troublesome Amsterdammer"), Amsterdam Fietst ("Amsterdam Cycles"), Kabouters ("Gnomes"), Fietsersbond ("Cyclists' Union"), Amsterdam Autovrij ("Car-Free Amsterdam"), and Wijkgroep de Pijp ("De Pijp Neighborhood Group"). Many weren't shy about putting their kids on the frontlines, and in 1972, the children of the latter were filmed demonstrating with signs, blockading entire streets to through traffic, and lobbying for safer "play streets" in their community, alongside their parents. Wooden crosses were planted in a nearby park to commemorate avoidable traffic fatalities. This outpouring of support was fueled by residents who recalled a time when their streets were about more than just moving and storing cars: "In Amsterdam, you had people with living memory of what streets were like when they were children," Dinca suggests. "That was enough to ignite that desire for a different urban reality."

While groups like the Provos, Stop de Kindermood, and Fietsersbond didn't necessarily coordinate their efforts, their concerns did converge, and they ended up reinforcing one another in the fight for a different type of city than what was being proposed. "They all had different perspectives," recalls de Lange, who participated in protests as a teenager. "Maybe they wanted more playgrounds for children, more safety for children, more space for cyclists, or more space for living. But most of it was focused of having a city that was not overwhelmed by cars."

A Choir of Divergent Voices

Elected officials heard the choir of divergent voices loud and clear, and in 1972 the city council decided, by a single vote, to scrap the motorway. "There were 22 councilors in favor of that plan," recollects de Lange. "But 23 were against it. So that really was a close battle. 'Urban renewal' had been rejected by the smallest of margins, and Jodenbreestraat and the surrounding community was saved from the wrecking ball.

Not wanting to lose the gathering momentum, activists ramped up their efforts. In a decisive act of solidarity, Amsterdam Autovrij, the Provos, and Fietsersbond organized a series of annual demonstrations leading up to a vital municipal election. In July 1975, 3,000 people on bikes took to the streets of Amsterdam to push for a more cycle-friendly city. The following summer, it was 4,000. In 1977, 9,000 attended, 3,000 of whom lay down with their bikes in Museumplein ("Museum Square") to commemorate the 3,000 annual deaths the Dutch people suffered at the hands of the automobile.

Provos leader Luud Schimmelpennink declared 1978 would be the fourth and final such protest, and it attracted an astounding 15,000 people. Four days later, their cause was given a tremendous boost with the election of a brand new council. And that autumn, a replacement *Verkeerscirculatieplan* ("Traffic Circulation Plan")—reducing motor vehicle traffic and parking, and prioritizing walking, cycling, and public transportation—was passed overwhelmingly by a vote of 38 to 7.

"The 1978 election was a real change," says de Lange, noting that these demonstrations were about more than just making noise. "The activists wrote reports to make sure people were informed about what to expect from various political parties, how they previously voted on mobility issues, and which politicians they should vote for." The Fietsersbond also published their *Fietsknelpunten Nota* ("Bicycle Bottleneck Report"), which identified problem spots in the city for cyclists, as well as possible solutions.

As soon as he was sworn in, the new deputy mayor for traffic and mobility, Michael van der Vlis, spoke to the protest groups and invited them to join him in a new bicycle-planning group that would include city officials and civil servants. "There were internal discussions at the Fietsersbond where they asked, 'Are we going to cooperate with the enemy, who had been so much in favor of cars?'" de Lange remembers. "But a large majority said, 'Yes, we should. We might have to make some compromises, but we see more advantage in cooperating than only demonstrating.'"

Thus began a productive and fruitful partnership between the Cyclists' Union and City staff, starting in 1978 with their collaboration on Amsterdam's first genuine cycling strategy, which built on the existing Bottleneck Report and Traffic Circulation Plan. "It was a vision about how you could achieve a bicycle city," explains de Lange. "What sort of infrastructure would you like? What kind of planning and policy do you need to accomplish it? It was a broad perspective on the bicycle city, with concrete solutions for problems that cyclists were facing."

Looking at Amsterdam today, it would seem the 1978 policy equated to thousands of kilometers of bicycle-specific infrastructure, creating a seamless network across the entire city. But the truth is actually a little more complicated and counterintuitive. This cycling utopia was built on traffic-calming rather than bike lanes. Instead of constructing separated cycle tracks on every street, officials started with speed-limit reductions, parking restrictions, through-traffic limitations, and lane narrowings and removals. This strategy proved to be incredibly fruitful, and—as biking flourished across the city—cycle routes were established in response to those increasing numbers, particularly on streets where bicycles regularly outnumbered cars. The spread of separated cycle tracks—which take more time, money, and political will—was more incremental, having been gradually built one at a time over many decades, although they now exist on nearly every major street.

Figure 5-2: Saved from the wrecking ball, Jodenbreestraat remains a street for people, moving tens of thousands of cyclists—and not cars—each day. (Credit: Modacity)

Dinca maintains this is a critical lesson for twenty-first-century cities looking to make cycling the primary choice for their residents: "Right now, a lot of cities are talking about making themselves better for cycling, but we can't talk about making them worse for driving." She concedes, though, that it is an easier conversation to have in a densely populated place like Amsterdam or New York: "It's really hard to push for speed reductions in an area that's so spread out, because everything is built around high speeds. This ends up being a huge barrier in car-dependent cities such as Los Angeles. Lower speeds are much more palatable when people are traveling shorter distances."

Much like the speed issue, compact cities offer a distinct advantage when it comes to encouraging a certain level of activism. "The role citizens play is really important," Dinca acknowledges. "There is so much community involvement in Amsterdam. Part of the reason why is because of the urban fabric—because of density, and land use, and people talking to one another—that makes it much easier for residents to get organized, to empathize, and even just to know what's going on and get involved." This is not to minimize the challenge other cities face if they try to replicate Amsterdam's success. "Every city is different, and has to find their own ways to improve the city," continues de Lange. "But I think what they can take from Amsterdam is the long-term vision and long-term policy that Amsterdam has been using. To build a bike city, it takes thirty or forty years, because you have to do it on almost every street."

Nevertheless, both Dinca and de Lange agree that it's not nearly as simple as copying-and-pasting these cycling strategies and expecting success. Says Dinca: "Part of it was luck, part of it was wisdom. But somehow Amsterdammers managed to realize for themselves and articulate what a livable city is all about. Every city has its own unique conditions and challenges. So it's not about making all cities like Amsterdam. It's about making them better versions of themselves."

Pulling Back the Curtain in the Social City

Move around the streets of Amsterdam today, and it's hard to imagine a time when bicycles didn't dominate the city's landscape. Truly, the success of the protests and activism of decades past is painted on the serene faces of thousands of cyclists as they move in an effortless ballet around their streets, enjoying the fruits of a social city. Ask any local about their cycle culture, and they will respond with a shrug, "What cycle culture? This is just what we do." The reality is that most of them take what they have for granted, spending little time thinking about how their lived experience is remarkable when compared with other cities around the world.

Until five years ago, Dr. Marco te Brömmelstroet was no exception. "If there is one moment I really started to understand what is special about the Netherlands," he says, "it was when I was invited by a journalist to observe peak rush-hour traffic in Amsterdam. It allowed me to stand outside of my behavior and see the dynamic occurring at intersections. That's when I realized how special cycling here is, and how it can provide a lens to rethink the language used in transportation planning. But it also made me realize I have a moral obligation to try to understand cycling, and to support those who bring it to other contexts by adding a critical perspective."

As academic director of the University of Amsterdam's Urban Cycling Institute, Te Brömmelstroet has spent a lengthy academic career studying urban planning, transportation, and geographic-information management. He ultimately describes himself as a planner with an interest in mobility and the relationship between the urban form and mobility behavior. "It's important to realize that, in the Netherlands, an urban planner is also a social scientist," he claims. "So I'm interested in how people make plans, and how they engage with different types of knowledge in doing so. Not so much the design or engineering of them."

Through the Urban Cycling Institute, he offers a summer-school program called "Planning the Cycling City," coordinated by Meredith Glaser (see chapter 4). Each session begins with a simple warning to the students who have traveled from around the globe to participate: If they wish to hold tightly to romantic notions of cycling, then they should walk away and continue to live in blissful ignorance. If they want to truly understand the unconscious nature of cycling in the Netherlands, they can watch as the curtain is pulled back, inevitably spoiling some of the fun. "Once you see it, you can't unsee it. But it's a necessary evil to help others understand," he advises.

For Te Brömmelstroet, the moral obligation to understand cycling pushes beyond simply sharing his knowledge with his students, recognizing that relying solely on the CROW Manual to solve Amsterdam's new bike-related challenges is wholly insufficient. To date, the city has managed to make things good for cycling within a car-dominated paradigm, but—now faced with increasingly bike-dominated environments—the manual has started to seem incomplete, and planners and officials need to start thinking outside the box. With researchers from the Urban Cycling Institute, including Glaser, he has spent years looking past quantitative data, instead studying the actual behavior of cyclists to inspire more behavior-based planning.

For instance, Te Brömmelstroet and his team—pairing up with the Copenhagenize Design Company—observed about 20,000 cyclists at 10 intersections throughout Amsterdam during morning peak hours, collecting data less focused on travel times and more on movements and interactions, observing stress levels via intercept surveys and ride-along interviews, and quantifying social interaction through monitoring eye contact. The goal of their work was to open up the thinking around data collection, offer a new visual language and a new set of metaphors to support creative solution-seeking, which would in turn lead to innovation, perhaps even fundamentally changing how transportation planners work.

Of the ten intersections studied—all of which are now being redeveloped using the data collected by Te Brömmelstroet's team—two of these solutions stand out as innovative steps forward in behavior-based planning. For example, the "funnel"—or "bag of fries" as it's now called because of its resemblance to a paper cone filled with French fries—is a busy intersection where a bidirectional cycle track crosses the street called Mr. Visserplein, at the foot of Jodenbreestraat. At the very site of the 1970s freeway fight, tens of thousands of cyclists now travel through that corridor, rather than the tens of thousands of automobiles that David Jokinen and his peers originally envisioned. Originally, on a red signal, cyclists would fill all the available space in the waiting area, spilling over into the oncoming lane as well as the adjacent pedestrian crossing, due to a lack of capacity. As the light turned to green, they would naturally organize themselves back into their designated space in a logical way, and carry on.

"That was a very good example where we could show the current conditions, but also show that it was putting people in a stressful situation they didn't want to be in, and they were solving the problem with the design by themselves," Te Brömmelstroet explains. And while users were addressing the issue directly, it led to the question: How could transportation planners design to cater for this natural behavior? In his opinion, their solution was beautifully simple: adapt the waiting area to suit to the behavior by redrawing a single painted line on the pavement. Instead of having two adjacent 4-meter- (13-foot-) wide cycle tracks, the City enlarged the waiting area to 6 meters (20 feet), and reduced the oncoming area to 2 meters (6 feet), creating a funnel that returns to the 4-meter width as it crosses the intersection. "This area is still used by the cyclists in the same way, but it fits the area much better. People are much less stressed and feel more supported by the design in their behavior."

Changes to the "bag of fries" intersection did not affect travel patterns for motorists, who enjoyed the same green time, so the design stayed within the confines of car-based engineering. On nearby Alexanderplein, however, the modifications would be more dramatic. After analyzing the behavior and stress levels of cyclists, along with the speeds of trams and cars, the recommendation required a bit more outside-the-box thinking: remove the traffic lights completely and "force" people to use eye contact and social interaction to dictate flow. Implemented initially as a trial, the now-permanent adjustment had no negative effects on travel time or safety, but instead created a whole new level of engagement. The former stop-and-go, high-stress experience was replaced with fluid movement, lower stress, and increased eye contact. When interviewed during the follow-up study and asked how they felt about the removal of the traffic lights, 10 percent of respondents said, "What traffic lights?"

The success of these projects affirms Te Brömmelstroet's belief in the importance of performing observational studies before, during, and after a project in order to build evidence of what is achievable in transportation planning with a more inventive mindset. "It's a great example of how the planning practice is changing through an innovative way of looking at reality," he says. "Something that's so mundane in the Netherlands, the fact that

Figure 5-3: Mr. Visserplein's "bag of fries" demonstrates that, when the CROW Manual is inadequate, behavior-based planning can fill the gap. (Credit: Martijn Sargentini)

we don't reflect on the act of cycling, is great. But it means we're not used to making policy for it, and that's really changing at the moment. People are taking it more seriously, and this banal thing of cycling is actually pretty special."

The City is continuing to move forward with the traffic-light project, commissioning the Urban Cycling Institute to study ten more intersections for potential redesign, now as part of their official *Meerjarenplan Fiets* ("Strategic Cycling Plan"). However, Te Brömmelstroet insists that agencies like the Fietsersbond and other cycling activists need to keep demanding more. "The City is doing the right thing at the moment, because the dynamics are there. More people are coming into the city and there are more people cycling," he suggests. "But citizen protests are necessary to push beyond responding to existing trends, and call for a long-term goal—where politicians and planners want to get to, not just solving problems right now."

"What we see is that we need to step up the recognition that if we think cycling is important—and I think there are enough reasons to think that— then we need to make an active effort in policy making," Te Brömmelstroet continues. "This means we need to have visions and strategies for the future." He points out that Amsterdammers take so much about cycling in their city for granted, meaning most politicians are unaware of potential threats, which aren't a subject of public debate. The approach so far has been to react to a disruptive problem after it becomes one—as has been the case for diesel-powered mopeds and speed pedelecs (electric-assisted bicycles that travel upwards of 45 km/h [28 mph]) using the cycle tracks—instead of looking forward and creating policies and visions to protect what it is the people want their city to be.

Te Brömmelstroet also notes that Amsterdam is experiencing similar pressures to those challenging other global cities: as economic growth increases, it creates a push for greater investments in public transportation and new innovations in the field—such as autonomous vehicles—many of which could have an adverse effect on cycling. As engineers focus on improving travel times and efficiency, there is the potential to lose something much more valuable—the cohesiveness created by social interaction within a city. "In the seventies, Amsterdam citizens demanded a social city designed for the people who live there and not the ones who travel through it," he recalls. "This needs to be the same discussion today. The public debate should not be confined solely to transportation, because that's way too limited in the face of these challenges."

Despite uncertainty around how future innovation will impact the cycling city of Amsterdam, Te Brömmelstroet remains rather optimistic. He has tremendous faith in the "swarm"—hundreds of thousands of people traveling through the city by bicycle, with little regard for how their movement has been made seamless and intuitive—as well as Amsterdam's proud cycling culture, however little Amsterdammers themselves may appreciate it. While he has lost his naïveté about the behavior of cyclists because his observational studies have revealed how truly remarkable and special cycling in Amsterdam is, he is grateful that the work of the Urban Cycling Institute can contribute to the romantic idea of cycling for his fellow citizens. "After all, I wish that everybody can keep experiencing this remarkable phenomenon unconsciously," he declares proudly.

How Tactical Urbanism Helps Bostonians "Demand More"

"As an architecture student, when you first get into school they tell you you'll never be able to see the city the same way again," explains Boston-based architect Jonathan Fertig. "But for me, I started to look at streets that way, more so than buildings. Streets and public spaces became the things where I asked, 'Why is the city like this? And why hasn't anything changed?'"

Through advocacy and activism, Fertig has spent the better part of a decade directing his passion towards demanding better public spaces in his hometown. After 10 years fully immersed in academia, the thought of simply putting in his 40 hours and then going home was just not enough, and it was the act of attending his first Critical Mass protest ride that inspired him to channel his "free time" into lobbying for safer streets.

"It was incredibly empowering," recalls Fertig. "I just remember feeling so energized riding while people yelled, 'Whose Streets? Our Streets!' Taking over a 15-meter- [49-foot-] wide street, curb to curb, in the middle of downtown and thinking, 'Wow, this is the first time the city feels like mine.'" The confrontational element of Critical Mass appealed to Fertig—known on social media for being outspoken with his opinions—and the event helped to identify a possibility for the streets he hadn't recognized before. While Critical Mass no longer exists in Boston, he uses online tools like Twitter to share ideas and photos from every city he visits with the hopes of inspiring change.

Like many professionals and activists in urban-planning and transportation circles, Fertig has found social media to be a powerful tool in promoting the good happening around the world, and it has given him a much greater understanding of what could be done for Boston. It has also been the ideal forum for challenging those content with the status quo, allowing him to be a consistent—and persistent—voice for advocacy groups that simply don't have the time or resources to dedicate to the online platforms. As @rightlegpegged, Fertig has found that access to a global audience with which to share images and concepts can be invaluable: he can tap resources previously unavailable to him and build a reputation for wanting more from his hometown.

Most unexpectedly, while he has developed a considerable online following within the urban planning and active transportation community, Fertig has also been able to use social media to gain access to politicians, with most of the Boston City Council following and actively engaging with him. "I've developed a relatively close relationship with the Boston Council president Michelle Wu, and I attribute that to my Twitter activism, which of course is a growth of my 'on the street' stuff," Fertig declares proudly.

The 'on the street' stuff is what Fertig is best known for, having made a name for himself through tactical-urbanism interventions in Boston. Like projects in Rotterdam and New York, his projects in Boston can be whimsical in their attempt to shed a positive light on what is possible, but their inception often comes from a much darker place.

On Friday, August 7, 2015, Anita Kurmann was riding her bicycle along a notoriously bad stretch of Massachusetts Avenue feared by many Boston cyclists—despite the paint-buffered bike lane—when she was struck and killed by a truck driver turning right onto Beacon Street. The City responded by promising to move quickly to improve safety for bicycles. In Fertig's opinion, they did not move swiftly enough. Spending $50 of his own money on traffic cones and flowers, he set them up along the painted bike lane, proving that with very little cost, an improvement could and should be made. Shortly after his installation—the pictures of which went viral on social media—the City stepped up and installed physical barriers, and thus began Fertig's adventure into the world of tactical urbanism.

Since that initial project, he has set up a crowdfunding webpage to raise money to temporarily upgrade other painted bike lanes in the Boston area, and he has solicited suggestions from others who would like to see such installations. His Provos-like "happenings" have included "People-Protected Bike Lanes": one-off events where activists gather in a row to form a "human shield" along a painted bike lane in order to draw attention to a substandard and exposed cycling facility.

The support he has received has far outweighed his expectations, helping to enable a lighthearted collaboration between himself and local artist Becca Wright, lovingly known as "Bikeyface" online. Wright is also famous for her tongue-in-cheek comics depicting North American bicycle culture, often challenging common misconceptions about the types of people who ride bikes—they aren't all "the fit and the brave" in her depictions. Over the course of nine months, she developed a selection of graphics in her signature style, which Fertig then printed at life-size and placed along various routes to serve as bold and highly visible reminders that drivers should, for example, "look for bikes before opening your door." While the City of Boston quickly removed them within 24-hours, they were so effective that the nearby City of Cambridge commissioned a re-creation of the series in more-permanent Dibond, an aluminum composite material, to be placed along some of their own cycling routes.

"I don't feel like any of this would have happened without social media," Fertig marvels, attributing the funds he has raised to simply being consistently visible online. And while his prominence has certainly played a role, he is also quite clever in how he uses social media, notably in the inception of the now widely used hashtag #DemandMore: "I used 'demand more' when I upgraded the first intervention at Mass Avenue and Beacon Street. I was at the office and somehow '#DemandMore' just sort of came into my mind, and I remember thinking that I should really stencil this. I plotted it out on our large-format printer, cut it out, grabbed a bottle of spray paint from the office, and just spray painted it on the ground on my way home."

Much to Fertig's surprise, not long afterwards groups in New York City and San Francisco started using the hashtag as well, and his simple message—that we should demand more from our cities and from our elected officials—started getting noticed and used online more generally. "It's nuts whenever I see it now, and it makes me so happy," he exults, and in fact Fertig has begun to use that hashtag for all of his interventions as a way to "tag" his work.

Figure 5-4: Jonathan Fertig's humorous collaboration with local artist "Bikeyface," which reminded Boston drivers to watch for cyclists. (Credit: Jonathan Fertig)

Since his first intervention in 2015, Fertig has pushed the City of Boston to take street safety seriously, with many of his illegal acts quickly followed by the official installation of physical barriers or other remedies. While he does view them as a positive step forward, Fertig worries there is potential to lose the plot, especially as advocacy groups and government agencies focus so much on the "Vision Zero" movement that aims for a road system with zero traffic fatalities or serious injuries. "I think the shift in bike advocacy over the last two years to use Vision Zero to advance things we were otherwise advocating for on the 'good urbanism' rationale is an interesting twist," Fertig explains. "I'm a little conflicted about it—it's obviously good when it comes to preventing deaths, but it's sort of taking up all of the air in the room. So in some sense there hasn't been as much room for discussion about why cycling for transportation is a good thing in and of itself." He points out no one is going to be against preserving and protecting lives, but the argument for better street design and reducing the number of cars in our cities, which would do far more to extend and enrich lives than building a few protected bike lanes, can get lost when the focus is on one particular outcome.

Fertig asserts that until attitudes around motor vehicle collisions change in North America, it will be impossible to achieve the Vision Zero goal across the continent. He notes at the time of the *Stop de Kindermoord* movement, around 450 Dutch children annually were dying as a result of car crashes, whereas in the United States of America, that rate is currently hovering at almost three times that number: a shocking 1,200 children. While the US population today is admittedly much higher than that of the Netherlands in the 1970s, if Vision Zero is to truly take hold, it can no longer be acceptable to sit back in complacency while over a thousand kids suffer horrific deaths each year with little or no consequence for the drivers at fault, all for the sake of convenience for the automobile.

In the meantime, Fertig continues to direct his passion for better streets into new tactical-urbanism activations. And he is seeing change, although not as fast as he would hope. "I think, in the long run, Boston can start to resemble Dutch cities. I don't see a lot changing in the next 5 to 10 years, but I think in the next 40 to 50 years it will happen," he reflects hopefully. He has watched the group of advocates and politicians in his corner grow over the last decade, which he attributes to the organizing power of social media. "Public meetings that people used to ignore are now in their faces, and you start getting the turnout," he says. "The ratio of people coming out to speak in favor of improvements is great, and we tend to overwhelm the dissenting voices now. I think we're all benefitting from, and trying to leverage, the power that this medium has, while attempting to make shit happen faster."

While change may be slow in Boston, compared with what advocates like Fertig would like to see, it is inevitable. The number of people moving into urban centers grows each year, and many cities are realizing they can't build their way out of congestion. Something has to give in order to accommodate the influx of residents wanting to use their streets more efficiently and more comfortably.

Cities like Amsterdam, which experienced very similar battles nearly 50 years ago, provide the proof that citizens can be the voice of reason and can demand action from their elected officials. Platforms such as Twitter and Instagram are offering a new way to share information beyond our immediate circles, delivering powerful before-and-after images of a city once clogged with cars that now puts people first. This helps even the most auto-centric cities realize that "If they can do it, so can we."

Fertig sees the combination of social media and tactical urbanism as part of an increased demand from citizens for better mobility options. This is especially true when it comes to creating safe space for cycling—a natural progression towards building human-scale cities that are better places to live, work, and shop. "At some point we are just going to have to understand the math: the most efficient way to move people through the city is to put them on bikes," claims Fertig. "I don't think it'll happen as soon as a lot of us would like, but I think it will in the next 50 years."

06 THINK OUTSIDE THE VAN

Bicycles offer a number of advantages in express delivery operations: they can bypass traffic congestion and make up to two times as many stops per hour than a delivery vehicle. The total cost of ownership over their lifetime is less than half that of a van. And crucially, they generate zero emissions, which reinforces our own ongoing program to minimize our environmental footprint and support city governments' efforts to promote sustainable city living.

— JOHN PEARSON
CEO, DHL Express Europe

With the distinct impression that cycling is simply part of the DNA of Dutch cities and people, it's easy to overlook the fact that one particular pedal-powered machine has not enjoyed the same enduring ubiquity as the *omafiets* and *opafiets*. For outsiders, it would appear that the traditional *bakfiets* ("box bike") has long been a staple of family life in the Netherlands, but in fact, the popularity of these impressive hauling machines is a relatively new rediscovery of an almost lost and forgotten design.

The *bakfiets*, or "cargo bike" as it is more commonly known in English-speaking countries, is a bicycle (or sometimes tricycle) with a large wooden box attached to the front, originally designed for hauling goods from A to B. Much like the original safety bicycle, which would later become the visual embodiment of Dutch cycle culture, the origins of the *bakfiets* lie across the North Sea in industrial England.

In 1877, John Kemp Starley invented the Coventry Rotary, one of the first chain-drive tricycles, opening up the possibilities for carrying cargo a decade before the safety bicycle hit the streets. Deemed less cumbersome than a horse-and-carriage, these freight trikes were perfect for tradesmen transporting bread, milk, and mail—pretty much anything that needed to be delivered from a business to the customer. As with the standard bicycle, these new machines eventually made their way onto Dutch streets, and while they enjoyed notable success in bigger cities, early generations of *bakfietsen* were more common in rural areas, largely due to fewer constraints around space for parking and storage. In the early days of the automobile, economic factors also played a role, as wealthier city dwellers were quicker to adopt the new motorized forms of transport than were their rural counterparts.

Despite a rise in car ownership in the early twentieth century, the *bakfiets* maintained its role in urban delivery, and it soon proved useful for trans-porting children as well—that is, until the arrival of motorized trucks, vans, and buses, and a corresponding increase in the size of goods being trans-ported. Where once the largest needs for hauling were daily groceries and small postal deliveries, there was now the need to deliver large appliances, which the bikes of the time simply could not accommodate. Similarly, in the late sixties, as families became smaller and car ownership spiked, the need for a specialized cargo bike—and the price tag that went with it—dwindled. In the following decades, the humble *bakfiets* all but went extinct, becoming a nostalgic storefront decoration recalling a bygone age, or ending up in a nearby junkyard.

Lost But Not Forgotten

Fast-forward to the late nineties, when after seemingly disappearing from existence for 20 years, the *bakfiets* began a quiet resurgence. But once again, the credit doesn't necessarily go to the Dutch. In nearby Denmark, industrial designers adapted the traditional tricycle to a sleeker, faster design, with a narrower front box and the two front wheels replaced with a smaller, single wheel connected to the front fork to improve maneuverability and responsiveness. Thus, the two-wheeled "long-john" style was born—the most recognizable brand being the popular Bullitt bike.

Around that time, Jos Sluijsmans—a lawyer who lived and worked in Nijmegen—was riding his recumbent bike to work every day and found himself wondering why so many of his colleagues were commuting by car when they had such great cycle infrastructure at their fingertips. That daily puzzlement eventually inspired a career change, with Sluijsmans dedicating his energy and passion towards cargo bikes. "At a certain point, I started to make a living by cycling, and one of the first things I did was start a bike messenger company," he recalls. "But I wasn't the type to ride a fixie [i.e., a fixed-gear bicycle, popular with messengers] with a bag across my chest, and I felt cargo bikes could be used to do the transport instead."

Serendipitously, the local SPAR—a grocery chain—had brought in a cargo bike for deliveries as a part of a pilot for the Province of Gelderland, but unfortunately, due to changes to the store's physical space, the grocer was no longer able to get it into the store. Sluijsmans saw an immediate opportunity and negotiated a deal whereby he would perform deliveries for the grocer as needed and, in exchange, would have free use of the bike for his own needs as a bike messenger and for his own personal errands.

Inspired by its Danish counterparts, the *bakfiets* has enjoyed a bit of a resurrection throughout the Netherlands. Sluijsmans recalls hearing stories of gatherings at Amsterdam's Vondelpark as early as 1996, where families would meet up with their cargo bikes and show off their ability to transport children. But their potential as freight vehicles was not really being discussed. Having used his own borrowed *bakfiets* for such a purpose, Sluijsmans felt a responsibility to demonstrate what was possible. "Internationally, you could see in other countries that people were using bikes more for fun than practicality, as we were in the Netherlands—usually by artists, the fringe, more creative people," he recalls. "I thought, in order to get people invested in cycling you have to make it more fun, more attractive, and of course showcase the designers that are using different materials to make bicycles."

Figure 6-1: A *bakfiets* rental scheme in Groningen, which—at €12 per half day (about $15 USD)—is a big hit with the student population, especially on moving day. (Credit: Modacity)

In 2012, after organizing a number of bike festivals over the years, Sluijsmans launched the very first "International Cargo Bike Festival" in Nijmegen. With just a few weeks to organize it, he invited a few of the people he knew with cargo bikes of their own, as well as a handful of companies that specialized in *bakfiets* design. He hoped that, if nothing else, it would be a fun gathering of like-minded people. "Some private companies came from around the country as well as twenty-five people with their own cargo bikes," Sluijsman remembers. "But what was remarkable is that not all of them were from Nijmegen." An additional but nice surprise was that, with no major promotion, he had also managed to attract three representatives from a Chinese electric-motor-design company. Not bad for what started out as a small event in the east of the country, far away from bustling streets of Amsterdam.

"I thought it was fun, so we tried to do it again the following year with a little more preparation and more people involved," Sluijsmans notes proudly. The International Cargo Bike Festival has since continued as an annual event, growing each year to include more vendors from around the world and attracting a global audience. It has also increased in size and importance through a strategic partnership with the European Cycle Logistics Federation, which was first founded at the ICBF in 2014. But as Sluijsmans points outs, despite its growth not only in popularity but also in the caliber of attendees—most notably shipping giants such as DHL—the welcoming spirit is never overlooked: "If you don't have anything fun happening, who is going to come to a cargo-bike festival other than people who already have cargo bikes?"

Sluijsmans is now a household name in the cargo-bike world, spending his time not only as the official organizer of the annual festival, but also a consulting member of the LEVV-Logic Project (Light Electric Freight Vehicles) with the University of Applied Science of Amsterdam, Rotterdam, and Arnhem-Nijmegen. He also acts as an advisor to both private companies and municipalities on how they can make things better for cycling. With LEVV, they strategically invest in areas that will create new possibilities for "green" logistics in city centers, and with his wealth of knowledge and experience, Sluijsmans sees a direct link to how cargo bikes are at the heart of such enterprises. The International Cargo Bike Festival has actually been able to provide the launching pad for many new innovations when it comes to reintroducing the freight bikes from the nineteenth century back to the forefront of today's transportation solutions.

"At the Cargo Bike Festival, we see a lot of parties that came two or three years ago with a dream of building a cargo bike, and now they are actually making the bikes and building a company around them," he recalls, noting that, not long ago, names like Yuba, Babboe, and Urban Arrow would be completely unknown except to diehard enthusiasts. But that's changing year by year. Sluijsmans is also continually amazed at the number of new companies that come to the festival from unexpected places—but with new ideas about how cargo bikes can change the game in both personal and professional transportation. "That's the interesting thing about sustainability now: there are more and more examples of companies making these decisions for economic reasons, not just to make the world better," he says. "That's bikenomics."

Taking a Great Idea and Making It Better

Like Sluijsmans, Urban Arrow founder Jorrit Kreek is another in a long line of individuals who probably never envisioned themselves leading a cargo-bike renaissance. A student of economics at the University of Groningen, he simply wanted to put his education to use, so, shortly after graduating, he moved to Amsterdam and launched an import company with his friends. One of those products was the Kronan bike: a Swedish-designed machine used by the Swiss army, first introduced to the Netherlands in 1999. "That's when I discovered that the bike is the best product you can sell, because it doesn't harm anybody," he explains. "It's so positive, it can replace a car and you can do almost anything on a bike." Kreek also quickly discovered that while the bicycle was a wonderful tool for transporting goods, it was wholly dependent on having the right accessories, something that became all too apparent when their best-selling add-on was the front transport rack.

Kreek continued importing the Kronan for six years, during which time he started a family. Like many, he invested in a cargo bike to transport his kids around town, opting for the common BakfietsNL model. But he found it clunky and awkward, and progressively difficult as his children grew in size and weight. "My entrepreneurial feeling was we should improve this, because more people could benefit if you made it more comfortable," Kreek states matter-of-factly. In 2009, after ending his venture with Kronan, he worked with designers to develop a cargo bike that fit three criteria: it had to be lightweight, comfortable, and—most importantly—electric-assisted. Made with an alloy frame, and a box composed of EPP foam rather than the traditional, heavy wood, the first prototype launched in 2010 was well received, beginning the story of Urban Arrow, and Kreek's entrance into the global cargo-bike market.

Competition between cargo-bike manufacturers is fierce, due in large part to a relatively small market. For most households, a cargo bike comes in handy until the children are grown and riding on their own two wheels. Also, the hauling capability, while attractive, is not necessarily suited to Dutch cycling culture, where practically every regular bike is fitted with front and rear racks, useful for carrying the daily grocery run or mid-sized purchases. Not to mention that the Dutch are renowned for finding inventive ways to carry nearly everything on two wheels—be it children, peers, luggage, and even the odd ironing board, to name just a few things.

In order for Kreek to set Urban Arrow apart from the rest of the field, he had to be innovative, and making his bikes lightweight and electric was not going to be enough. The solution: a modular design that adapts to the user's needs. "The modular design was meant to allow people to swap the front frame," explains Kreek. "Once the kids are big enough to bike themselves, they can swap to a more compact cargo bike."

Unlike the more-traditional *bakfiets*, the Urban Arrow has a frame that is manufactured completely separate from the box portion, of which there are several design options to suit a variety of uses. Kreek acknowledges that while the goal is to be a successful company financially, this electric-assisted, modular system is about providing viable transportation alternatives to the private automobile. "Everybody is aware that we have to change our way of transport in cities, and that is something we want to be part of at Urban Arrow—to be a game changer in urban mobility," he explains.

Since its launch, Urban Arrow has grown exponentially, with dealers throughout Europe and even as far away as Australia and New Zealand, but Kreek specifies the US market as the one they plan to put effort into growing in the coming years. The trouble is that it's still a relatively small market compared to Europe; Kreek is well aware that in North America cycling is regarded as more of a leisure activity than a daily routine, making a cargo bike unnecessary for many households. Interestingly, however, Kreek sees potential not in large cities like New York City or Los Angeles, but rather smaller, less densely populated areas.

Figure 6-2: The Urban Arrow's lightweight, electric-assisted, modular system adapts to the user's needs. In this case, it's the family minivan. (Credit: Urban Arrow)

With North American cities still playing catch-up on the quality and connectivity of their fledging bike networks, the average citizen will likely be much less comfortable cycling next to their kids on the busy streets of a major urban center. As a result, Kreek anticipates the Urban Arrow filling a gap in smaller, more-suburban areas where road conditions for the daily school run can be calmer and more comfortable. He is optimistic that the American market will develop in time: "In the end it will happen in the United States as well that our cargo bikes are everywhere," Kreek predicts confidently. "In Amsterdam, it was just 15 years ago that you would be an exception to be riding your kids around in a cargo bike. It will take some time, but it will grow."

Back home in the Netherlands, Urban Arrow is quickly building a reputation as the "Rolls Royce of cargo bikes," spreading the cargo-bike culture across the country, and not just as a family bike. Knowing the historic roots of the *bakfiets*, Kreek saw the potential for Urban Arrow's modular systems to change the way freight is being moved through crowded urban streets. "The average delivery vehicle, whether car, van, or truck, takes up space, pollutes, and is inefficient in terms of energy, time, and cost," he explains. "Cargo bikes provide an option to replace those trips with a compact, adaptable solution that is not adding to the congestion on the streets." The interchangeability of Urban Arrow's design meant that, without changing the main frame of the bike, they could provide cargo options for all types of deliveries.

As Kreek soon realized, that would include one of the largest retail chains in the Netherlands. "We were aware Albert Heijn [the largest Dutch supermarket chain] were thinking about having an alternative for their delivery vans, to make it more green and electric, so we reached out to them and proposed they take a look at what we can offer," Kreek recalls. "They looked at our existing product line and told us they needed to be able to carry 40 crates of groceries on the bike, which our current model couldn't accommodate."

Understanding the incredible potential this opportunity had, Kreek strategized with one of his designers, and two weeks later he presented a three-wheeled model, its front portion resembling more car than bike. As required, it could carry 40 crates. Their biggest challenge was the fact that bike technology presently maxed out at a hauling capacity of 150 kilograms (330 pounds), but a 40-crate shipment could weigh up to 400 kilos (880 pounds). "It was a good idea to look over the fence and say, 'Hey, maybe we should use some car technology in our bike,'" Kreek recalls. The innovative thinking has paid off, with Albert Heijn testing out their new fleet of delivery bikes on the streets of Amsterdam and looking to expand to other markets in the near future.

This new, greatly expanded model has also brought Urban Arrow to the attention of other large organizations, including maintenance providers for multinationals like Coca-Cola, many of whom typically don't need to carry more than their toolbox from service to service. They also worked with the Dutch motoring association ANWB to adapt a model that provides roadside assistance to cars, as well as one for PostNL—the national postal service—who have committed to deliver emission-free in 25 cities by 2025.

"We are at the tip of the iceberg, with lots of changes coming in the next three to five years," boasts Kreek, who recognizes that much of his success comes from partnering with the right individuals. "Our engineers weren't trained in cargo bike development because that industry didn't exist yet. We are the front-runners in that respect." While the future looks very bright for Urban Arrow, Kreek is aware there is still work to be done. Their bikes are helping families and businesses move through cities in green, healthy, and more-efficient ways, but they are not without their own logistical problems—space, cost, and, even comfort, despite e-assist. Pedaling an e–cargo bike on a gloriously sunny day presents no difficulty, but once rain or snow sets in, such trips become more challenging. "On paper they are always very nice, but in practice there have to be some hurdles to overcome to make it smooth," he admits.

"Even so, it's great to be a part of that change to more green transportation," he's quick to add. Whether through the growth of the North American market share, or their expansion into urban delivery solutions, Urban Arrow is expanding the possibilities in urban mobility. Their modular design means that they are in a position to adapt as the needs of their markets change—be they personal or business needs. Kreek's entrepreneurial spirit has allowed him to recognize opportunity when it is presented, while maintaining his idealism regarding the societal benefits that come from bicycles. He has certainly seen the value of bikenomics, and he's reaping the rewards. "Smarter mobility is good for families," he asserts, "but also for business."

Bakfiets *on Broadway*

While the *bakfiets*'s elegance, versatility, and functionality captured the imagination of North American advocates for many years, like the plain Dutch bike, it remained difficult to access outside Europe. If cargo bikes were to proliferate on this side of the Atlantic, it would take an emerging cycling city to adopt and adapt them, on a retail, manufacturing, and cultural level. Perhaps unsurprisingly, one of the first North American settings to wholeheartedly embrace their potential was America's self-proclaimed "Bicycle Capital," the Pacific Northwest city of Portland, Oregon.

Compared to the rest of the continent, Portland is the poster child for postwar smart growth—the product of a freeway revolt, an urban-growth boundary (the first of its kind in the United States), strategic light-rail investments, and a 300-mile network of traffic-calmed neighborhood bikeways and painted lanes. The latter has resulted in the highest bicycle mode share—about 6 percent—of any large American city (over 300,000 residents). Most notably, with an image shaped by the hit mockumentary television series *Portlandia*, the Rose City has successfully branded itself as a vibrant and innovative bike-centric destination, attracting inventive talent and creative energy from across the country.

"Portland was definitely fertile ground for something like cargo bikes to happen," notes Jonathan Maus, who has been covering the local bike scene since 2006 as publisher and editor of *BikePortland*, a blog dedicated to all things bicycle. "When you have such a crazy reputation, and a brain trust of people who come here because of bicycling, you create fertile ground in the same way that Silicon Valley attracts a certain type of person. Portland was really known for its bicycling, so it was just a matter of time."

In the summer of 2006—the early days of his website—Maus was walking along Broadway in northeast Portland when he stumbled across a woman pedaling an authentic *bakfiets* imported from the Netherlands. The woman, who had recently transferred from Nike's Amsterdam offices to their world headquarters in nearby Beaverton, posed for a photograph that Maus immediately posted on BikePortland.org under the title "*Bakfiets* on Broadway." At the time—in the early days of social media, blogs, and Google images— the idea of a front-loading cargo bike was extremely novel to his readers, and the post attracted a significant amount of traffic. "I think they'd do very well in Portland, and I have a hunch we'll be seeing more of these around town in the future," Maus predicted in his entry, unaware that the post itself would eventually serve as the genesis of his city's nascent cargo-bike scene.

"That post really got a lot of attention," remembers Maus fondly. "It hit a lot of people in Portland orientated towards bicycling in an exciting way—

the tinkerers and creative types." Four of those readers were friends and married couples Dean and Rachel Mullin, and Todd and Martina Fahrner, who immediately identified a gap in the local retail market. "A light bulb went off in their heads," suggests Maus. "They started clicking around the Internet and realized that no one is importing these things into the United States. They end up rolling open their garage door, finding a source, and bringing in these cargo bikes, and the rest is history."

Since opening up in June 2007, Clever Cycles has cleverly cornered the transport-cycling market, selling a selected range of cargo and family bikes (including the Urban Arrow), upright city bikes, folding bikes, electric bikes, and kids' bikes. This practicality has been good for business, and they've expanded their family-friendly shop to a total of 7,000 square feet. In 2012, *Bicycle Retailer and Industry News* named them the "Best Urban Bike Shop" in America. "Clever Cycles was the pioneer for what I called Portland's 'Dutch Bike Invasion,'" says Maus. "It wasn't just the cargo bikes, but all things Dutch were coming over. They established themselves with the *bakfiets*, and were able to start a business that's still around and actually quite successful."

Once Clever Cycles had solidified their reputation as a supplier of imported cargo bikes, it wasn't long before the domestic frame builders and manufacturers got in on the action. Longtime friends Philip Ross and Jamie Nichols emerged from this ecosystem of garage tinkerers to form Metrofiets in 2007, selling *bakfiets* for both personal and commercial use that were designed and built in northeast Portland. "Their story was important on a lot more levels than Clever Cycles," proposes Maus. "Clever were importing a foreign product, with all the associated costs that go with that. Then Metrofiets set up a shop in a residential neighborhood, and were making them just as good, if not better than, the Dutch version." Where several other custom builders had tried and failed—citing cost and complication as insurmountable barriers—Ross and Nichols perfected the process, making it clear that the Portland market had matured to a point where it was ready for its own bespoke cargo-bike manufacturer. To Maus, this was a signal to the community that these freight bikes could be lighter, more responsive, and even more beautiful than the *bakfiets*—and could be made locally.

Figure 6-3: Portland's Metrofiets designed and built this custom delivery bike for Trailhead Coffee Roasters; it doubles as a portable café. (Credit: Jonathan Maus)

Portland also lays claim to the nation's first "Disaster Relief Trials," a family-friendly event that has brought the community together every autumn since 2012. In anticipation of "the Big One"—the earthquake that will inevitably rock the Cascadia Subduction Zone, imperiling Portland—a group of enterprising citizens arranged a scavenger hunt in which participants pick up medical supplies, food, water, and even "injured" people by cargo bike. Local and statewide agencies have since gotten involved, witnessing firsthand how the aftermath of any natural disaster can benefit from nimble vehicles immune to the concerns of clogged streets, energy shortages, and flooded cars. "It is to cargo bikes what tactical urbanism is to activists, in that it gives them a real-life scenario to see how it goes, and to see what goes wrong and what goes right," Maus suggests. "And with weather-related disasters on the rise, it's super-relevant."

The natural next step in Portland's maturing cargo-bike culture was to start shifting freight via more efficient means, beginning with the formation of B-Line Sustainable Delivery in 2010 by Maine transplants Franklin and Kathryn Jones. Acting as a "viable, alternative, clean-energy" distribution grid, B-Line's fleet of custom-built, electric-assist tricycles provide a smart "last-mile" solution to businesses across the city. "Their growth and sophistication over the years has been impressive to watch," asserts Maus, "to the point where now they've established themselves, both geographically and strategically, at the center of what I hope is the future of cargo transport." B-Line cemented that position in 2015 by setting up shop in "The Redd on Salmon Street," an 80,000-square-foot production and distribution campus housing local food enterprises, along with their growing pedal-powered logistics network.

B-Line isn't the only company providing this type of delivery service. Portland Pedal Power is another owner-run organization, founded in 2009 by Ken Wetherell, who designed and built his own custom cargo-bike enclosure. Their fleet of 14 delivery bikes brings food and products to businesses in the busy downtown core, having found a niche of catering lunch to the local tech industry. Maus believes both success stories speak volumes about the need to rethink how we move freight in our cities, a possibility not ignored by larger corporations like UPS, which, in late 2016, announced that Portland would be the site of their first electric-assist-trike pilot scheme.

The vision of far fewer trucks traveling in the public realm is indeed enticing, and one Maus imagines could provide the impetus for real and lasting change. He points to the August 2017 death of 41-year-old Tamar Monhait, killed by a left-turning truck in an industrial area just a few blocks from B-Line's headquarters. "If it was picked up by the right advocacy effort, the safety improvements that come with pedal-powered freight could really catch on," he declares. "The kinds of trucks we're currently using are far too big for our cities. They are incompatible with human life. And there's definitely a political urgency building around that issue."

The act of parking and unloading these trucks is perhaps an even more substantial obstacle to human-friendly streets, and it is now often done in the very facilities designed to protect cyclists. Maus brings up the City of Portland's "Central City in Motion" plan, a comprehensive strategy to improve transportation in the core that is still in development but is due to be officially unveiled in June 2018. According to his sources, dealing with truck loading and unloading zones is one area where staff are doing a lot of hand-wringing, which he fears is resulting in a great deal of compromise. "If there was an advocacy plan on the table that said 'Let's get rid of these trucks and use cargo bikes instead,' that could actually have a big impact," he argues. "That could set the stage for some major leaps forward."

As far as the cargo bike has come in recent years, Maus believes it has reached a point where it needs government-led policy and street design to achieve its optimal capacity. "If some city were to really embrace its potential, and come out as a leader, they stand to gain a lot. It just seems so ripe," he submits. "We reach these roadblocks in North American cities where people can't think big when it comes to changing how we use streets, what we do on our streets, and the general culture of our streets. There are a lot of mental roadblocks that lead to physical roadblocks."

And much like the case of e-bikes, sales of cargo bikes for personal use also stand to plateau without the proper incentives and infrastructure in place. "The type of people most likely to want to use cargo bikes are also the type who want better infrastructure for their biking," he says. "And they don't have that. So sales are going to hit a ceiling to some degree." Maus recollects his partner Julie test-driving a Clever Cycles *bakfiets* for a period of several weeks, only to decide against purchasing it for a variety of reasons, including the lack of accessible and secure parking, and the absence of curb cuts on many streets.

But Maus is particularly excited by the powerful combination of electrification and cargo biking, and reckons Portland is well placed to lead the charge towards a quieter, cleaner, safer, and healthier future. "In addition to the people who are evangelistic about cargo bikes, Portland has an exciting scene of people who see electrifying them as a natural fit. And those two worlds have merged," Maus asserts. "It's really transformative what electric-powered cargo bikes can do to a city."

Reimagining the Shipping Container

In addition to UPS's rather modest entry into the world of cycle logistics in Portland, German distribution giant DHL are rolling out their own last-mile solution on the streets of five Dutch cities (as well as locations in Austria,

Belgium, and Germany), in the hopes they can scale it up to global proportions in the coming years. Much like Rotterdam embraced the shipping container as a concept that revolutionized international shipping, DHL is betting that a smaller, cargo-bike-sized container will do the same for urban freight. Acting as the primary last-mile vehicle in that visionary new model is the "Armadillo," a four-wheeled pedelec developed in Gothenburg, Sweden, by Velove CEO and cofounder Johan Erlandsson.

While completing his "half-PhD" in engineering focused on energy and the environment at Chalmers University of Technology in Gothenberg, Erlandsson was particularly interested in motor-vehicle technology, especially the emerging trend of electric- and hydrogen-powered cars, until one day he came to a stark realization: "I recognized that if you run the numbers, and look at how many resources you have to put into a car, and the energy supply needed to propel that car, the idea that every household should have one or two cars doesn't fit into a sustainable budget."

A 2006 visit to Copenhagen opened his eyes to the world of cargo bikes, inspiring Erlandsson to return home and replace his Toyota Prius with a Nihola front-loading tricycle. As he began to research the topic of the velomobile—a weather-protected, human-powered vehicle with low wind resistance—he got the idea of combining it with the carrying capacity of a cargo bike, creating what he imagined would be a "car killer." "You would have almost all the qualities you get from a car," he suggests, "but in something that uses so little resources and energy that it's actually something everyone on Earth could own and use every day. It's a factor of 15 to 20 times more efficient than a car, while doing the same transport work of short trips in cities."

Erlandsson used a sustainability discussion board he was managing at the time to lead an online brainstorming session, which culminated in an in-person workshop with 10 advisors from various professional backgrounds who settled on a basic set of qualities they would like to see in such a vehicle. "After that, my dad built the first prototype, which was on almost no budget. Less than €500 [$620 USD]," he recalls. "It was a four-wheel bike. No suspension or e-assist. But it was extremely stable and relaxed."

While he was chasing down grant money, the promise of this first prototype was enough to convince Erlandsson to simultaneously start his own bike courier business in Gothenburg, which eventually allowed him to scrape together enough funds for a second prototype, this time with a €5,000 budget ($6,200 USD) that equipped it with front suspension and electric assist. Around that time, however, Erlandsson realized that, while the professional market for a "car killer" already exists, the personal market still needs time to develop. "The price level is such that if you replaced a van with this bike, it would be considered relatively cheap," he explains. "But if you sold this to regular households, it would be considered a very expensive bike. So this is when we started to focus more on developing the vehicle for professional logistics."

This renewed push was boosted by an unexpected windfall of €25,000 ($31,000 USD), half of which came from state funding and the other half via contest-prize money from a local energy company. That injection of capital was enough for Velove to hire engineers from the Dutch company Flevobike—specialist producers of velomobiles and two-wheeled recumbent bicycles—to refine Velove's design into a market-ready product.

Fearing the Armadillo might make cycle paths less attractive to new and existing users, Erlandsson stressed to the engineers that the final design must be congruent with existing bike infrastructure. And at 86 centimeters (34 inches) wide—a little narrower than most family cargo trikes—and 160-centimeters (63 inches) high—no taller than an adult on an upright bicycle, they definitely accomplished that. "The whole reason why we do this is for sustainability reasons, and we want people to move from cars to bikes," he insists. "We've done everything we can to minimize the impact on other cyclists."

In the spring of 2014, when Flevobike were in the process of building Erlandsson's third prototype northeast of Amsterdam, he decided to accept Jos Sluijsmans's invitation to attend the International Cargo Bike Festival 100 kilometers away in Nijmegen. There he made a connection with a representative from DHL, which would further refine the design of his invention. "At that time, the box looked like a container, but it was bolted onto the back of the bike," Erlandsson recalls. "They asked us, 'Can you make this detachable?' We said, 'Sure we can.' So we solved the detachability, and it became a modular container." Unbeknownst to Erlandsson, DHL was already exploring containerization with smaller boxes that fit onto the front-loading Bullitt bike—but the back-loading Armadillo suddenly opened up a world of fresh possibilities.

Under their current delivery model, DHL Express utilizes terminals strategically located adjacent to the nearest airport, where packages are sorted and loaded onto the shelves of large vans, which transport them directly to the receiver's doorstep. Under the new, experimental model, parcels are loaded directly into the shipping containers based on their destination, and then several containers are picked up and stacked in a central location by a single truck. Each container is then transferred to a cargo bike, which can then run a route of up to 40 parcels, returning the empty container when the deliveries are completed. These empties are then sent back to the airport terminal by van, traveling anywhere from 20 to 40 kilometers away from the city center.

Figure 6-4: Velove's "Armadillo" cargo bike in action, complete with detachable container, which DHL hopes will revolutionize urban freight. (Credit: DHL Express)

"The pure business argument is that you get high productivity in con-gested cities, because you're faster on a cargo bike in a dense city center," explains Erlandsson. With up to double the productivity—twice as many parcels delivered per hour with a bike than a van, and a lower cost of owner-ship—the expense of purchasing the vehicle, maintenance, fuel, etc.—one can easily understand why DHL are keen to expand this model outside of its testing phase, which includes the Dutch cities of Alkmaar, Breda, Houten, Nijmegen, and Utrecht. That's not even considering the substantial pub-lic-relations benefits, such as a viral March 2017 *Tech Insider* video viewed over 6.5 million times. "They had never seen anything like that," declares Erlandsson.

Knowing a good branding opportunity when they saw one, DHL Ameri-cas even went as far as to ship an Armadillo—rebranded as the "Cubicycle"—to New York City in July 2017, opening the New York Stock Exchange, and participating in the closing ceremony of the penultimate race of the 2016–17 "Formula E" electric street racing season. The bike will remain in Manhat-tan, and—if approved by regulators for US streets—will lead the first urban containerization pilot on North American soil.

With the Cubicycle now front and center on DHL's marketing materi-als, it looks likely to be a major player in their climate strategy, aiming for net-zero transport-related carbon emissions by 2050, with 70 percent of all last-mile deliveries made by "clean" modes of transportation (either electric van or bike). Considering the increased productivity and decreased operating costs, it is highly likely that deliveries will be made by bike where it is pos-sible, and motor vehicles will only be employed as a last resort.

In addition to an aggressive scale-up plan based on their growing rela-tionship with DHL, which includes a second production line in the Czech Republic, Erlandsson is consulting with several cities about overhauling much of their urban freight into a consolidated, container-based system. "They see this as the way forward, as a way to transition to a more respon-sive and city-friendly logistics industry," he explains. In his hometown of Gothenburg, for example, city officials are testing a publicly run enterprise that combines packages from two private companies in a small electric van. That single vehicle replaces two large, half-empty trucks roaming sensitive areas such as the city center, allowing the same person to simultaneously deliver packages from two different carriers. Today, this solution requires the costly intermediary step of re-sorting and loading the parcels—but if containerization were to be incorporated, the streamlined operational costs would decrease significantly.

For Erlandsson and the Velove team, the end goal is about finding exciting new efficiencies in an industry handling larger and larger amounts of freight, especially with the seemingly boundless growth of e-commerce. "We think it's important to understand when a cargo bike is the best option and when it's not," he proposes. "We're definitely not suggesting that we're replacing all of the trucks and vans in a city. But we want to replace them when their use is ridiculous, when you use a huge van or truck to deliver very small items. There's a lot of that inefficiency today."

07 BUILD AT A HUMAN SCALE

Our revenue is healthy people, less traffic, and beautiful living.

— FRANS JAN VAN ROSSEM
Head of Bicycle Programming, Utrecht

Affectionately known as "the biggest village in the country," Utrecht's unique charm can be explained, in part, by its medieval buildings, ancient canals, ornate bridges, and cobbled laneways—a rich, 2,000-year history, all contained within compact boundaries. In its infancy, Utrecht marked the northern edge of the Roman Empire, whose fortifications are commemorated today with a series of decorative steel rails embedded in its streets signifying the borders of that ancient fortress. In the centuries that followed, the outpost evolved into the wellspring of Christianity in the Netherlands, as well as an important trading hub—due to its strategic location along the former shore of the River Rhine—protected by a surrounding moat. But in its twentieth-century haste to transform itself into a modern city, its stunning beauty was nearly sacrificed at the altar of the automobile, an "improvement" that was reversed once residents came to the stark realization that a car-first city and a human-scale city are mutually exclusive.

Despite being on the Nazis' chopping block, Utrecht managed to make it through the Second World War relatively unscathed, narrowly avoiding the devastating fate suffered 60 kilometers (35 miles) west in Rotterdam. "It was scheduled to be bombed flat by the Germans the day after Rotterdam," recounts Dutch cycling ambassador and *BicycleDutch* blogger and filmmaker Mark Wagenbuur, who then adds, "That's the reason the Dutch capitulated." The surrender of the Netherlands led to five difficult years of German occupation.

After the war, this sleepy provincial town started to think bigger, beginning with the expansion of the Jaarbeurs, a million-square-foot exhibition and convention center next to the Centraal railway station. "That became an economic engine for the city, which started to develop and get ideas," explains Wagenbuur. Planners and politicians were desperate to redevelop the medieval inner city, which was seen as inaccessible and incompatible with their aspirations. "Even road designers were looking jealously at Rotterdam, because they had a blank canvas, saying, 'They can start anew, and we can't,'" suggests Wagenbuur. "So they decided, 'Well, okay, our city wasn't leveled, so we may have to be bold and do it ourselves.'"

In 1956, the Utrecht city council approved a memorandum by German traffic engineer M. E. Feuchtinger entitled *Toekomst Oude Stad* ("Future of the Old City"). Despite his own counts showing that 74 percent of the traffic moving in and out of the city center was of the two-wheeled variety, Feuchtinger called for the demolition of the medieval core to make way for wider streets and parking garages. His calls also included filling in the historic moat to create a wide ring road around the perimeter of the city.

Unlike Amsterdam, which immediately ridiculed and dismissed the proposal to abolish its canals, Utrecht consented to Feuchtinger's foolishness, paving over part of the moat, the Catharijnesingel, with a 1.5-kilometer- (1-mile-) long, 11-lane stretch of motorway in 1968. This road was designed to access the adjacent Hoog Catharijne, a huge North American–inspired shopping mall and office complex that opened five years later, in 1973. "They wanted the roads from the US. They wanted the malls from the US," laments Wagenbuur. But these altogether out-of-scale developments, along with the demolition of cherished buildings and the clear-cutting of trees, were enough to give residents a firsthand view of exactly what they were giving up. "People started to think differently," recalls Wagenbuur. "They were reacting to plans they saw being built, and reacting to new plans that were being developed. They said, 'Wait a minute. What we see is already horrible enough. Don't go on.'"

According to Wagenbuur, the tight urban fabric of ancient Utrecht was fundamental to its citizens' rejection of certain modernist principles of urban planning. "There was no way to keep the buildings and to have a car city. It was either–or," he says. "Cars are so space-inefficient that you can't have a city that's on a human scale, and also a car-oriented city at the same time. If you have the latter, it's the former that suffers."

The Hoog Catharijne project ignited a vociferous opposition from residents and preservationists who opposed any further alteration to the medieval buildings and waterways. Eventually, they attracted the attention of the Dutch culture minister Marga Klompé—the Netherlands' very first female minister, and a graduate of the University of Utrecht—who in 1972 decreed Utrecht to be "a protected cityscape" of cultural and historic significance, thus formally safeguarding it from the bulldozers. As in Amsterdam, many of the social movements opposed to car-centric modernization represented divergent interests but, without even realizing it, were all working together for the greater good. "Some people were saying, 'Don't tear down my home,'" explains Wagenbuur. "Others were saying, 'Don't cut down my right to cycle.' Still others were saying, 'We shouldn't ruin these monuments.' But essentially they all said, 'We want a liveable city.' That's only what we see now, in hindsight."

The year 1974 saw the publication of Utrecht's first traffic-circulation plan that actively considered people on bikes and public transit, proposing a dense, citywide network of physically separated cycle tracks. But most importantly, these infrastructure investments were complemented with measures that made driving a car incrementally more difficult and less desirable, including on-street parking reductions, the construction of bus-only lanes, and traffic-calming streets to a 30-km/h (19-mph) limit.

Nowhere is that more apparent than on Vredenburg, the city's major east–west arterial, next to Hoog Catharijne. In 1962, it was subjected to one of Feuchtinger's early road-widening projects, leading to the construction of two bus lanes and four car lanes, along with a pair of unidirectional cycle tracks. Proving the adage "If you plan cities for cars and traffic, you get cars and traffic," the street was soon clogged, much to the ire of bus drivers,

Figure 7-1: After the Second World War, Utrecht's delightful, human-scale city center was nearly sacrificed at the altar of the private automobile. (Credit: Modacity)

traffic wardens, and thousands of other users traveling that corridor. Within 10 years—after the relocation of a mall parking entrance—single-occupant vehicles were all but banished from the street, with one eastbound lane all that remained until Vredenburg was made completely car-free in 1996.

A significant portion of the cycle traffic using Vredenburg today is headed to or from Centraal Station, a testament to the harmonious connection between bikes and trains in the Netherlands. Utrecht's compact size and status as the country's busiest rail hub—due to its central location—means that this relationship is stronger than anywhere else, creating some unique problems that require some unique solutions. The city was, in fact, home to the country's first underground bike-parking facility, built in 1938. Demand has since skyrocketed, and officials are currently building a number of large and ample *fietsenstallingen* ("bike parking lots") in and around the city center. In 2001, Utrecht was the natural choice to serve as the pilot city for OV-Fiets, the national bike-rental scheme: a convenient service that has expanded exponentially to strengthen the powerful bike–train combination.

Over a period of 30 years, officials in Utrecht have gone from believing the bike would become extinct to beginning to cater to cyclists, but Wagenbuur insists that it wasn't until the early nineties that cycling found its rightful place near the top of the transportation hierarchy. "Only after the adoption of 'Sustainable Safety' and the CROW Manual did cyclists get a place in our system," he argues. "Then you see a big improvement in the standard of cycling infrastructure. So it took a very long time."

The period between 1994 and 1998 was a particularly fruitful one for active transportation in Utrecht, as Groen Links ("Green Party) vice-mayor and traffic alderman Hugo van der Steenhoven took over the reins. He worked closely with activists in the Fietsersbond to build out much of the cycle track network proposed in the 1974 circulation plan. Van der Steenhoven also oversaw the construction of numerous strategically placed *buurtstallingen* ("neighborhood bicycle-parking facilities") across the city—empty shop fronts that were reclaimed and retrofitted to act as secure community bike storage. The City of Utrecht now owns and operates 36 such *buurtstallingen* in residential neighborhoods. Last but not least, he was responsible for the aforementioned decision in 1996 to finally close Vredenburg to private automobiles. That same year, Van der Steenhoven instructed City staff to begin studying the possible restoration of Catharijnesingel from motorway back to waterway, a vision that would ultimately take over two decades to be realized.

If spatial constraints helped Utrecht retain its human scale after the Second World War, in stark contrast to Rotterdam, then these same constraints will also drive its mobility and planning decisions for the next century. "Utrecht is the fastest-growing Dutch city," explains Wagenbuur. "It's getting bigger, but the territory is fixed." So absorbing 40,000 new residents in the coming years will mean that more-efficient modes of transport must be prioritized out of necessity, a reality that puts the automobile at the bottom of the list. "It's the lack of space that forces this city to think differently," says Wagenbuur. "More traffic of a type that is space-consuming is just not possible in the same area, using the same roadways. That simply cannot happen."

"It's Really About Space-Efficiency"

Just how does an ancient city like Utrecht plan for an influx of residents and still maintain their human scale? As Wagenbuur points out, despite its historic bones, the city hasn't been immune to the same auto-centric thinking seen in cities around the world, and backpedaling from those ideas hasn't been a quick fix.

"It took about five decades from when Utrecht really embraced the car as king, and now we are looking for alternatives—especially in our spatial planning—to send another message," explains Lot van Hooijdonk, deputy mayor for the City of Utrecht, who is in charge of the mobility and sustainability portfolio. "From the seventies until now, especially in the urban context, we really developed a new story."

In early 2016, Utrecht established a new mobility policy that centers on space-efficiency. Van Hooijdonk and her colleagues understand the importance of accommodating future growth without sacrificing the efforts of their predecessors. That involves looking at space in relation to the transportation hierarchy used across the Netherlands: pedestrians first, then bikes, then public transit, and finally, at the very bottom, the private automobile. Via street-narrowing, improving cycling facilities, establishing pedestrian-only spaces throughout the city center, and reducing vehicle parking, the message is clear: "The car is not king here."

Nevertheless, achieving space-efficiency in Utrecht is about reimagining not just the streetscape but also the buildings that border the streets, all in an effort to change behavior. "What we try to do in the new developments—where you have the chance to reorganize, where people start new routines—is to try to influence the choices in their behavior," Van Hooijdonk explains. She notes that this is particularly attractive when looking at solutions in Utrecht's nearby suburbs. "I think one of the great opportunities we have is also to make the regional infrastructure and network better," she says. "While the city itself grows to 400,000 inhabitants, for the region it's 800,000 to 900,000, so that's double the number of people where you can attempt to influence their choices, and try to seduce them to take a bike over a car."

In order to convince higher levels of government to co-fund bike-infrastructure projects, Utrecht has opted to tout them as "no regret" solutions. As the Province of Gelderland discovered with the RijnWaalpad (the "Rhine–Waal Path"), these investments will not only make conditions better for people who already cycle, they'll also provide an attractive alternative to those who frequent the overcrowded roads and railway system, especially with more and more people looking to e-bikes as an option for longer journeys. Van Hooijdonk is quick to acknowledge that the bicycle is not the only solution available, and she stresses that they also hope to improve public-transportation options, which are contingent on funding from the regional and national government.

Back within the city limits, making space for the projected 10 percent population growth in a city so constrained by history and geography requires a deeper understanding of the link between housing and how people get around. As Van Hooijdink submits, they are now exploring ways of reducing the amount of auto parking in new developments in order to influence a conceptual transition from car ownership to mobility as a service: "We are trying to build between 9,000 and 10,000 homes, a density unfamiliar for us in Utrecht—making it a really urban space." As for car parking, she says, "We have three scenarios: the most conservative is 0.7 cars per house, and the most progressive is 0.1 cars per house, which basically involves only car-sharing." She recognizes that, even in a locale where the bicycle is so readily accepted as the most practical and efficient transportation choice, the real question is whether it is actually possible to convince so many new homeowners to forgo car-ownership altogether. It requires spending some political capital, but the City of Utrecht will forge ahead and see where the idea takes them.

"Of course, they all include very good bike facilities. That's the basics," asserts Frans Jan van Rossem, the head of Utrecht's bicycle programming. And those fundamentals are being taken very seriously at Utrecht's Centraal Station, which currently sees more visitors annually than the national airport at Amsterdam Schiphol, an impressive 88 million. Travel anywhere throughout the Netherlands by rail, and making a stopover or connection in Utrecht is almost a certainty. While the station is a thoroughfare for many rail passengers, Van Rossem is quick to point out it is also a key destination for many residents of the city and surrounding suburbs. "If you look at Amsterdam, they have a lot of smaller stations around the central station so they can handle lots of traffic," he says. "But in Utrecht, the suburban train stations are not very big, so everything concentrates pretty much in the center, which is more or less a natural phenomenon, and that's why so many people use the central station."

Van Rossem posits that the volume of people traveling to the station is in direct relation to the scale of the city. Because Utrecht has been built out from its moated center, even the farthest outskirts of the city are just eight kilometers (five miles) from Centraal Station, making it accessible to nearly every resident via 20 minutes on a bicycle or public transportation. At the same time, with very little space available for car parking in the city center, driving becomes an incredibly impractical and expensive choice. "We recently did a study that found that Utrecht has the highest percentage of people getting to work by bike and train: 51 percent of all people working in the city are getting to work by some combination of bike and train," Van Rossem reveals.

Just imagine that: over 200,000 people traveling from all points of the city and congregating in the center, all by bicycle. Van Hooijdonk points to two specific factors that have directly influenced that transportation decision. First and foremost, Utrecht is the only one of the four largest Dutch cities without a streetcar system to complement the national rail system. Their public transit system consists solely of buses, which tend to be less attractive and less desirable than a sleek tramway.

But more importantly, it was a national decision made 15 years ago that really impacted the city's future: "In the Netherlands, they decided we would improve the international rail lines to Belgium and Germany, and therefore the stations on these corridors should be improved. The Hague, Rotterdam, Amsterdam, Breda, Arnhem, and Utrecht have all had new train stations built as a part of this decision," she explains. "For Utrecht, the national decision to renew the train station fell into a bigger municipality project to renew the whole station environment, and nowadays we are realizing it. At this point, I think they have made the right decisions to make big bike-parking stations as a part of the whole context of these large renewals of the station, the municipality office, and the large mall next to the station."

By the beginning of 2019, Utrecht will be home to the largest number of publicly available bicycle-parking spaces in the Netherlands: a total of 22,000 public spots spread across several lots on the east and west sides of the station. This includes a single, spectacular 17,000-square-meter (184,000-square-foot) facility with spaces for 12,500 bikes, which—when complete—will be the largest such structure in the world. This project is financed by the provincial, regional, and municipal governments, with operational costs covered by the Nederlandse Spoorwegen (or NS, the national rail company), the rail infrastructure company (ProRail), and the City of Utrecht.

But as Van Rossem points out, those sizeable operational costs will be incredibly difficult to cover without any sort of revenue stream. "That's the conversation happening now. We think it's good that the train passengers using these facilities also pay a part of the cost in operating them, but we don't want to ask them to pay €0.50 [62¢ USD] each time," he clarifies. "If you do that, they'll think it's too much hassle." He and his colleagues are pushing to have a small charge integrated into the concession fee for all public transportation agencies, including the buses. "This is an ongoing national discussion. We have to find a solution to finance these bicycle parking facilities," Van Rossem notes. "It cannot be that just the city government has to pay for them."

In Utrecht, a city where local policy is to continue reducing the number of car-parking spaces in the center, finding that local revenue is an increasing challenge. "In the development of fewer cars and more bikes in the city center—at this time, with it being paid parking—the cars are bringing the City millions of euros every year," says Van Hooijdonk. "So if you want to get rid of these car-parking spaces and give them over to bike parking, you get rid of something that makes money for something that costs you a lot of money. It is a financial challenge," she concedes.

The solution bears some resemblance to Paul de Rook's plans in Groningen, but on a larger scale. In order to build a new project or redevelop an existing structure, businesses not only have to provide car parking in the new facility, but also bike parking. "I don't think many other cities in the Netherlands have implemented this, and it's pretty much nonexistent abroad," says Van Rossem. He points to several new developments in the city center— including new municipal offices and the World Trade Centre Utrecht—that, combined, will provide 11,000 private spaces; the City will then negotiate to make a number of them publicly available. "We share the costs," he explains. "They invest in these new facilities, and then we do some of the operational duties."

Van Rossem sees this as an advantage to both parties. Shop owners and people who work in the city are realizing the importance of having access to good off-street bike-parking facilities because there are so many bikes crowding the footpaths. Business owners have been asking the City to solve the problem, which, he argues, they cannot do on their own. "We need cooperation. Those bicycles in front of their shops are also customers, and they don't want to chase them away. So they recognize the need."

Scalable Solutions for the Most Bike-Friendly City in the Netherlands

Looking at Utrecht from afar, it is easy to scoff at their struggles. What most officials wouldn't give to be that city—with half the population cycling to work each day, with bike-parking problems, and with a delightful, human-scaled city center. But that small scale has started to create conflict with the ever-increasing share of people traveling by bicycle. Their challenge moving forward will be building on these successes while also increasing population density, all without sacrificing the livability, comfort, and historic beauty residents have come to expect of this special place.

Vredenburg's transformation from a car-choked traffic sewer to the single busiest cycle path in the Netherlands should be lauded as an amazing, forward-thinking achievement. On a daily basis, Vredenburg now sees an average of 34,000 cyclists moving east and west through the center, reaching a peak of 41,000 within one particularly busy 24-hour period. But as the city and the surrounding suburbs grow, those numbers are expected to increase further, eventually becoming unsustainable.

Figure 7-2: Utrecht's Vredenburg moves 34,000 cyclists a day over the reclaimed Catharijnesingel, previously an 11-lane stretch of motorway. (Credit: Modacity)

"It's partly a product of our new suburb," reveals Van Rossem. "We have a very large new suburb to the west, and the university is to the east, so if people want to go to the university by bike, they choose this route mainly because it is the most direct from Leidsche Rijn to the university. Also, because the railways run predominantly north to south, there are not many other possibilities to cross the rail tracks, so that's why this route is so important—because there are not many other options."

Along with Utrecht University, the new Science Park has become an attraction for international businesses and is currently the largest destination in the country inaccessible by rail. Projections are that it will employ at least

30,000 people, where the only options for getting in and out every day are the car and the bicycle—the latter being the main option. Both Van Hooijdonk and Van Rossem recognize the need for a scalable solution, and while a tram-line to connect it to Centraal Station is under construction, speculation is that the new tram will be at capacity the day it opens.

To ease that congestion, Utrecht has embarked on a project that was ini-tially a measure of practicality, but has since put them on the map as a place to marvel over the Netherlands' latest piece of "bike bling." As the neighbor-hood of Leidsche Rijn grew on the west bank of the Amsterdam–Rijn Canal, residents were becoming increasingly vocal about adding a bike crossing so they could get into the city without traveling miles out of their way. Just across the canal sat an old school in need of replacing, and the City saw a unique opportunity: build a new school that would serve as an on-ramp to the bridge, complete with a cycle path on the roof! "The Dafne Schippersbrug and the OBS Oog in Al School is a great project," says Van Rossem enthu-siastically of the new bike-pedestrian bridge and its innovative on-ramp. "I think it has to do with the tradition in Dutch society to work together to solve a problem, and also we don't have a lot of space, so we are always looking for space-efficient solutions. I think it's really brilliant."

Since opening on April 3, 2017, the number of travelers crossing the bridge has been steadily increasing. What was long just a line on a map has been transformed into a vital link to the city center and surrounding ameni-ties. The neighborhood around the school has also benefited tremendously, and Van Rossem points to a sense of revitalization in the community. Of course, the new school is the source of great pride for its students and staff, many of whom get to use the bridge on their daily travels, and pedal down off the roof of the building to their classrooms!

While officials look ahead at solutions for accommodating residents as they move through the city, they are excited about the completion of a monu-mental project that will inject a newfound emotional connection to the place they call home. After two decades of planning the removal of the much-despised "motorway from nothing to nowhere," the City is set to reopen the Catharijnesingel canal as a complete and connected waterway by the year 2020. Van Rossem, who grew up in Utrecht, has nothing but negative

Figure 7-3: The on-ramp for Utrecht's Dafne Schippersbrug allows cyclists to roll up onto the roof of the newly opened Oog in Al School. (Credit: Modacity)

memories of the former motorway. "It was a very dead piece of city," he recalls vividly. "There was no fun; it was a very good place for people to use drugs, especially in the tunnels for goods delivery. I think that's one of the reasons they started to rethink what to do with the space. It was not attractive and scary to get to by bike."

Now, Van Rossem looks forward to the positive ways that restoring the canal will change his city for the better, becoming a great gathering space not only for tourists but also for locals who once saw it as a wasted piece of the public realm. As with Amsterdam's famous canals, tourists and residents alike will be able to travel by boat around the core, reviving a long-forgotten romantic connection to a place that was long cold and desolate. As for Van Hooijdonk, having moved to the city as an adult, she is excited for the new possibilities that the revived waterfront will bring to Utrecht, noting that it is something that is already being taken for granted by locals: "I think most people can't imagine anymore what it used to look like just a few years ago."

All in all, Utrecht seems to be staring down the challenges of future growth with optimism and innovation, but this is not happening without its naysayers. Just as with the demolition of cherished buildings and trees in the 1960s and '70s, residents are wary. "It has spurred a debate because Utrecht has been growing really fast," admits Van Hooijdonk. "Just a couple of decades ago we only had 200,000 citizens, so I think we're experiencing growing pains. Some people say they don't like the growth; it's not their city anymore; where's the human scale? I think we're maybe beyond that discussion now, but 10 or 20 years ago, that was the prime debate." She also feels that while they've made progress, there's still much work to be done: "I think the funny thing is we still have a long wish list, so we don't think the city is done improving things for cycling. The local discussion is not about satisfaction, but about what we still need to achieve."

This is a common sentiment voiced across the Netherlands, and, to be sure, a healthy dose of cynicism helps to ensure politicians don't rest on their laurels. While urbanists and advocates in places like Britain and North America look in awe at these cycling havens, their residents are still not satisfied—but international recognition helps. In 2017, Utrecht was listed second on the global Copenhagenize Bicycle-Friendly Cities Index, edging out local superstar Amsterdam; an accolade Van Hooijdonk doesn't take lightly. The ranking inspires pride in the city she has happily served for some time, and it makes her optimistic about the future.

Van Rossem, meanwhile, looks to the recent past, recognizing that Utrecht's success has roots in decisions made before his and Van Hooijdonk's time: "We are proud of what we have achieved, but we haven't just done it ourselves," he admits. "There's a big team working on it, and our predecessors did a lot of work. But I think we can be proud as well. A lot of people say, 'We can really see you're working on new cycling infrastructure now.'"

"There is a new renaissance for cycling in the Netherlands," submits Van Hooijdonk. "It's seen in the interest and attention of the public. I hope it creates new fronts and we'll have many new projects in the future, because we think we're not done yet."

Building a Better Market Street

Measuring just 11 kilometers (7 miles) by 11 kilometers, and surrounded on three sides by salt water, it could be argued that San Francisco is one of North America's few human-scale cities. With a population of 870,000, and a density second only to that of Manhattan, it has many distinct advantages, including its compact nature, mild climate, and a long and storied history of social activism, dissent, and protest. Not only does it lay claim to the modern environmental movement, it is also home of the very first Critical Mass protest ride, which began as a modest gathering in 1992 but has since spread to cities around the world as a tool to mobilize and garner political support. But to many who want their city to become an even more walkable and bikeable place, that heightened level of engagement and awareness has become both a blessing and a curse.

"If you contrast San Francisco with New York, New York tends to have a very strong mayor, and a long tradition of bold civic leaders, from Robert Moses to Janette Sadik-Khan," explains Jeff Risom, partner and US managing director for Gehl, a global, Copenhagen-based urban-design consultancy. "San Francisco is more grassroots, with a weaker mayor system, and a lot more civic engagement." In that environment, what Risom refers to as "the Tea Party of the left" has come to monopolize the city-building conversation for several years—be it on zoning, housing, or transportation. While the city prides itself on being socially progressive and environmentally minded, this combination has created a breed of uncompromising liberal NIMBY ("Not In My Backyard") so far to the left that they've actually become hyperconservative, and government officials have become paralyzed by the many disparate progressive stakeholders and their vast resources.

For example, in 2006, the San Francisco Municipal Transportation Agency (SFMTA) was slapped with a lawsuit by "concerned citizen" and car-free activist Rob Anderson, who—bizarrely—opposed their bicycle network plan on the grounds that removing driving lanes and parking spaces would worsen the air quality. The suit resulted in a court-ordered injunction that prevented the City from building any new infrastructure until a four-year, $1-million review proved that the plan complied with the California Environmental Quality Act, and would not result in an increase in carbon emissions. A judge eventually lifted the injunction in 2010, but not until the SFMTA had fallen woefully behind on their bike plans.

Yet the City of San Francisco was innovating in unexpected ways, creating groundbreaking permitting programs built on grassroots civic tactics like PARKing Day. It was in that dynamic atmosphere that Gehl—after working on the pedestrianization of New York's Times Square during the Sadik-Khan era and later opening an office there—opted to open a second US office in San Francisco. In 2014, they joined forces with Rebar, a local art and design studio responsible for the first PARKing Day. Gehl had already been working in the city for three years on the Better Market Street project, which was stalled due to an extensive multi-year environmental review process. Market Street stands as the city's most iconic and frequented thoroughfare—a grand 38-meter- (120-foot-) wide boulevard stretching 4.8 kilometers (3 miles) from the Embarcadero waterfront on San Francisco Bay to the hills of Twin Peaks in the geographical center of the city. It is also San Francisco's transit backbone, where a majority of the city's municipal transit (MUNI) bus and underground train lines converge with the Bay Area Regional Transit (BART) system.

The planning process for a Better Market Street began in 2009, when state and federal funding was offered to repave the corridor in order to improve transit speeds and reliability. Like the initial incarnation of Utrecht's Vredenburg, Market Street moves a tremendous number of people—over a quarter million on public transit and hundreds of thousands on foot each day—but suffered from the same inefficiencies, where trams and buses were forced to mix with cyclists and single-occupant vehicles, often causing them to fall behind schedule. Design concepts had been developed and rejected. A solution satisfactory to all stakeholders seemed unlikely, and the project threatened to languish forever.

That is, until Risom and his team got involved. Gehl was the urban-design lead of a large consortium of internationally recognized design firms selected in 2010 to redesign Market Street; the team included Perkins+Will, CMG Landscape Architecture, David Parisi, and Nelson\Nygaard. "Market Street is basically the transit and infrastructural backbone of the city," explains Risom. "It's the spine where all the transit lines converge, and then diverge to the various spokes." Along with Market Street's status as a transit workhorse, Gehl also had to respect its requirements for public space, for local businesses, and for private vehicles—and Gehl had to listen to the 12,000-member-strong San Francisco Bicycle Coalition. "Because of that highly contentious nature, and the impending intensive environmental review of major capital projects, it lent itself to an incremental prototyping approach," Risom reveals. "Rather than a grand plan, it's more about the grassroots, scrappy, do-what-you-can style. That's what San Francisco culture has been about. The challenge was to still combine that scrappy, do-what-you-can style with a bold vision."

The Intersection Center for the Arts, which bills itself as "the oldest alternative nonprofit art space in San Francisco," had held a small prototyping festival in 2014 that captured the more constructive side of San Francisco's spirit. But they had to fight through the considerable red tape (over 80 permits were needed to activate a disused block-long section of a street adjacent to Market). To pull off another prototyping festival, this time along several blocks stretching the length of Market Street, the group would need outside support. Risom looked to leverage Gehl's outsider's perspective together with this local energy and creativity, and so he introduced the Knight Foundation to the concept of reimagining Market Street thorough prototyping, long familiar to local organizations like Yerba Buena Center for the Arts and its executive director, Deborah Cullinan, and the head of urban design at the Department of City Planning, Neil Hrushowy. In 2015, they all collaborated on a much larger prototyping festival along the entire length of Market Street. For just a few days, residents could experience how a more inviting, inclusive, and livable street felt, and how it could function as both destination and thoroughfare. "That was really important, because it allowed a lot of people to understand what the street could become, in a much more playful and visionary way," Risom explains, recalling the temporary sidewalk, cycle track, and seating treatments that were tested during this time.

Later that year, looking to extend the spirit of that short festival to a more permanent vision for the street, the cohort teamed up with Mayor Ed Lee's Office of Civic Innovation. They established a number of "Living Innovation Zones"—envisioned as "streetlets": slightly larger variations on the "parklet," located on the sidewalk—along Market Street. There they provided "blank canvases," either vertical frontages or rooftops on underutilized portions of the street, where permitting rules would be streamlined and partners were encouraged to be creative in providing space for walking, cycling, seating, and gathering. More partners came to the fore, including the Yerba Buena Community Benefit District and the San Francisco Department of Public Works.

Through these initiatives, despite San Francisco's notoriety for its red tape, Risom and the cohort of collaborators made it clear to everyone involved: This was a bureaucracy-free zone. "That was the idea, to provide a space where some of the rules could be easily bent, and where we could actually try stuff," he recalls. "But not purely run-of-the-mill, boring planning stuff. We said, 'Hey, let's partner with fun folks like the Exploratorium [San Francisco's Museum of Science, Art, and Human Perception] and see what they would like to do with that canvas.'"

These activities and events, including pop-up libraries, ping pong tables, and interactive art installations, started attracting a wide range of citizens— inviting more of the kind of meeting, learning, and playing usually reserved for parks or plazas, but rarely seen on streets—and a new vision for Market Street began to emerge. Not only did this eye-opening event appear to get the Market Street scheme back on track, but the data collected by Gehl before, during, and after the prototyping festival helped decision makers revise and refine their goals. "The data we collected was one of the first times someone counted all modes of traffic at the same time: transit users, drivers, pedestrians, and cyclists, all mapped simultaneously," Risom discloses. "We also measured how people experienced the street. Not just moving through the street, but spending time on it: sitting, standing, playing. We call them 'stationary activities.'" That shift from quantitative to qualitative data has been critical, and Risom's team spent a fair amount of time training City workers in their methods: "Now the City does a lot of that collection themselves, and they use that data about street life and use to actively inform their decision-making process."

In July 2017, a final design (inspired by Gehl's work, but ultimately produced by the City) with a $604-million budget was revealed to the public, including generous 6-meter- (20-foot-) wide sidewalks, 2.5-meter (8-foot-) wide protected bike lanes, and dedicated public-transit lanes. While this 3.5-kilometer (2.2-mile) stretch won't be completely car-free, it restricts through traffic sufficiently in the hopes that, like Vredenburg, that inevitable next step can be made within a decade with minimal blowback.

Figure 7-4: The new vision for San Francisco's iconic and much-frequented Market Street includes eight-foot-wide protected bike lanes. (Credit: San Francisco Public Works)

In addition to building a better Market Street, the SFMTA is also in the process of enhancing the Embarcadero, the 4.8-kilometer (3-mile), at-grade, bayside corridor that was the site of one of America's most prominent and dramatic freeway removals, albeit, unlike Utrecht's careful canal reclamation, not by choice. Built in the car-mad 1960s, the Embarcadero Freeway was an elevated, double-decker monstrosity that partially collapsed during the Loma Prieta earthquake of 1989, suddenly reconnecting downtown San Francisco and the surrounding neighborhoods to the city's waterfront, including popular attractions like the Ferry Building, Fisherman's Wharf, and adjacent beaches. In light of the decision-making paralysis that plagues the city, it seemed unlikely politicians would ever slate this highway for demolition, as replacing the structure would have been far too costly. But Mother Nature forced their hand—and San Francisco is a more vibrant, connected, and enjoyable place because of it.

Now, as they embark on a visionary redesign process similar to the transformation of Market Street, city officials and advocates have sky-high hopes for the Embarcadero as a world-class public space that prioritizes people over automobiles. This will likely include the calming of through traffic, a significant increase in the size of spaces to walk and gather, and the conversion of painted bike lanes to ones that are fully protected.

But Risom warns against oversimplifying and over-romanticizing the idea of freeway removal, particularly in the North American context. "There haven't been too many situations like the Embarcadero, where it was caused by natural disaster," he suggests. "I think it's hard. We have a glorified idea that if we demolish or repurpose this big piece of infrastructure, everything will be okay. But it's really expensive to do. It's a real challenge to activate large spaces like that in an inviting and human-scale way. It's a lot better just not to have built it in the first place."

Many of Gehl's clients in smaller US cities such as Akron, Ohio, are now trying to figure out what to do with the interstate highways bisecting their city centers, and, unfortunately, Risom has no easy answer for them. "They think, 'Oh, we'll make the High Line,'" says Rison, referring to a popular reclamation of an elevated freight rail line in Manhattan. "'Or we'll do this or that.' But we have to tell them, 'No you won't, because this is eighteen times the scale of the High Line, in an area with one-twentieth the population density.' We've got to be really careful with that. It's romantic and it's interesting. But I think it's way more challenging than we imagine."

Whether it's Market Street or the Embarcadero, San Francisco is well on its way to building more-inclusive streets, but Risom fears that cultural inertia may be too difficult to overcome. "I think San Francisco has a huge NIMBY problem. They are paralyzed, crippled by their fear of change and the vested interests that don't want things to change. So it's a huge problem. For the city to become more affordable, more has to be built. So it handcuffs cities in this lose–lose situation," he laments.

But he certainly sees prototyping and data collection as two valuable tools in surmounting that inertia: "Our hope is by getting good data, we can do some 'myth busting' to get on the same page and have different views, but rational conversations about what is actually happening out there. That way we can address natural fear of change, and minimize risk by doing learning as we go. If we can combine that iterative approach with a bold vision and high ambitions for creating invitations for all people," he says, "then we're on the right track."

08 USE BIKES TO FEED TRANSIT

The bicycle is not an alternative for the car. Neither is the train. The combination, though . . .

— MARCO TE BRÖMMELSTROET
Academic Director, University of Amsterdam Urban Cycling Institute

As a country, the Netherlands—it could be argued—is one of the most well connected in Europe. Their fast and frequently running rail network, consisting of almost 7,000 kilometers (4,350 miles) of track, ensures that no matter where someone lives or works, they are in close proximity to a station. It therefore comes as no surprise that the nationwide system serves over 1.2 million passengers each and every day, half of whom bookend their train travel with bicycle rides—chiefly because of the practicality evidenced by Utrecht's massive investment in bike-parking facilities, which nevertheless some suggest will fail to provide enough capacity, even when complete.

Referred to as the bike–train combination, this remarkably seamless, door-to-door system draws the envy of transportation planners outside the Netherlands who are clamoring to find ways to get their residents to choose other, more-efficient modes over the single-occupant vehicle. But how those Dutch officials got to today isn't nearly as straightforward, and—as with many policy decisions across the country—has more to do with responding to existing conditions, rather than proactively planning to affect them. "I don't know if 'coincidence' is the right word," speculates Roland Kager, "but I believe that, while of course each individual component of the bike–train system has been planned, there was never serious policy that envisioned it as a whole, and consequently constructed it. If something happened, it was more of a reactive policy, and that was true until recently."

Roland Kager is a data analyst and transport consultant at Studio Bereikbaar in Rotterdam, and has been a key player in studying and documenting travel data related to the bike–train phenomenon in the Netherlands. During his postdoctoral studies, he took on the enviable task of analyzing bike–train records to answer two questions: Can you create an accurate model that reflects the differences between the bike–train combination and any other merging of transportation modes? And why is that relevant? Up to that point, no one had ever really taken a hard look at the synergy between cycling and public transit, and while this study started as a mere side project from a broad national research program, it quickly became a focal point because of the incredibly valuable and interesting dynamics he uncovered among public transit (in particular trains), cycling, and land use.

"It's quite difficult to fill in multimodal trips: short walking trips, short biking trips, or various combinations in a data survey. This whole spectrum is not really covered, and it's mostly geared toward unimodal and longer-distance trips such as those by car," Kager explains. "The *korte ritjes*, or small trips, are what makes a city function, and also why bike-train-based mobility works very different from car-based mobility. You need to be much more selective in the places you visit and how you combine modes. The primary constraint is not distance but connectivity." Kager's studies revealed how cycling typically offers a meaningful choice between stations and services by allowing an individual to personalize their transit system. By looking at such effects, researchers begin to understand how cities, cycling, and transit systems function together in a web of interactions that are often overlooked, either in managing the present conditions or in planning for the future.

Thanks to his research, the national government and national rail company (NS) are now more hands-on in addressing challenges, though those issues are not always easily identified. When a car is stuck in traffic, or there is a problem with the road network, it is readily visible. This is not always the case when it comes to bicycle travel. "If a link is missing on your cycle route, you can easily adjust your trip with no drama," Kager argues. He points out that is the inherent strength of the bicycle as a mode of transport—it can grow its modal share quickly without serious constraint or becoming a drain on the existing infrastructure. But that is also an innate weakness, keeping serious problems under the radar for a long period of time. "That changed in the early 2000s, when a new dynamic started with the urban revival," he says. After that point, the Dutch bike–train system started to receive more attention, quickly becoming a main policy theme. The focus is on what the existing systems are, what they could be, and how to capture value from them to pay for further investments.

According to Kager, a key strength of the Dutch approach to the bike–train combination lies in its scalability. Because the trains themselves run at capacity, there is simply no room for bikes on the carriages, and for that reason, they are not permitted on most routes. In countries such as Denmark, where investments have been made to allow passengers to bring bikes on board, there is only a finite amount of growth the system can absorb. While just 15 percent of Danish train users cycle to the train, that number has surpassed 50 percent in the Netherlands, with nearly 600,000 bikes across the network each day. When Denmark's numbers approach a fraction of that level, they will face a serious problem: how do you scale back on something that customers have now come to expect—especially if no other alternatives are offered?

For the Dutch, this has resulted in enormous bike-parking facilities at stations throughout the country, similar to those seen in Utrecht. "As a user, you would be happier if you could just take it for granted that your bike is safe where you left it at the station, with another bike available at the other end," explains Kager. And with the addition of OV-Fiets in 2004, as well as third-party bike-sharing options, the "last mile" of any door-to-door trip is becoming increasingly seamless. "The strength of public transport is its efficiency," he continues. "If you cancel out this efficiency, then it's a dead end."

Adaptability and scalability aside, Kager points out the true success of bike–train is not how each mode operates in isolation, but how they perfectly complement one another. Culturally, bikes have been ubiquitous on Dutch streets for over a century, and the rail network has been transporting people from region to region as long as residents can recall, but the two modes working together to form a comprehensive system is what makes it unique.

Figure 8-1: A sea of bikes outside Rotterdam's Centraal Station, a secondary overflow area to the main 5,190-space facility built below the station in 2013. (Credit: Modacity)

"People often claim the bike brings passengers to the station, but I also insist the Dutch rail system is a crucial factor in explaining the bike culture," he says. "We wouldn't have good transit if we didn't have good bicycle infrastructure. It goes both ways."

Kager recalls growing up near Amsterdam, and the rate of cyclists at that time being one of the lowest in the country. The city itself was dirty and dangerous, and many were leaving urban centers for a cleaner, quieter, safer existence. But just as in regions across America, there has been a marked reversal in these migration patterns over the past two decades, with people and socioeconomic activity returning to city centers in hoards, bringing with them densification, an increase in cycling numbers, and in response, better transit options.

"Around the year 2005, cities flipped from going downwards to a positive energy, and now into a self-reinforcing loop with cycling and transit modal shares," Kager explains. "As cities are getting stronger economically, how do you get to the city? By train. How do you get to and from the station? By bicycle. If you live in that city, how do you move around locally? By bicycle." He further submits that as demand increases, bike and train facilities improve, along with other sustainable modes (like public transit), and cities become increasingly attractive places to live or to set up businesses. As a result, the demand on cycling and transit options that connect to and from surrounding cities and villages increases, having a "knock-on" effect in the neighboring areas, and perpetuating the cycle.

Kager does note that while the bike–train arrangement operates in a loop, cycling plays a vital role—which he refers to as the "magic hand"—in that it has the potential to self-organize "thick" transit streams in between an existing cluster of stations. Public transit on its own operates on fixed corridors— a train or tram can only operate on existing tracks, buses mainly on major streets where passengers are more likely to gather. The only way to deliver quality service is by having a method to feed people into that fixed stream from a larger area, something that the bicycle does exceptionally well.

As seamless as this seems, complications arise when looking at the urban– rural divide emerging across the country. Only 20 percent of the Netherlands is considered urban—now with strong socioeconomic growth, increased housing prices, and stronger connections within city limits and surrounding centers. However, this leaves the other 80 percent of the country faced with the choice of either connecting to the existing system at a pace matching current trends, or transforming their own systems in a way that meets the needs of local residents and businesses.

"The question becomes: How do we connect or transform that 80 percent to fully participate in emerging urban lifestyles and economies?" Kager says. "Bike–train is the toolbox that can help, because it delivers urban accessibility." Growing municipalities such as Amsterdam, Rotterdam, and Utrecht can absorb only so many new inhabitants. By making selective investments in bike–train infrastructure, officials can help the remaining 80 percent to participate in the expanding urban system in a more balanced way, and—at the same time—deliver a more robust, complete, and nationwide option, available to everyone.

Solving the "Last-Mile" Journey

Narrowing the urban–rural divide by providing better mobility options will take years, and because of the sizeable scope, the effects will likely not be felt for a generation. In the more immediate future, a tangible solution will be to solve the dilemma at the destination station: how to make it easy for passengers to make the "last-mile" journey by bicycle. As Kager noted, while stations of departure see upwards of half of their passengers arrive by bike, fewer than a third of those same people leave the station on the other side in the same manner.

Kees Miedema, program manager of transport integration at NS, admits that the importance of this final link was only realized in the early 2000s, coinciding with the explosion of growth in urban centers. "We learned 15 years ago that choosing the train as a mode of transport is only worthwhile when you look at the complete perspective of the trip from door to door, not only from station to station," he explains. "A big reason why people don't choose the train is because they think it's a hassle to get to the station, and an even bigger hassle to get from the station—in a town you may not know—to your destination."

By surveying their passengers, NS learned that while they were mostly quite comfortable while on the trains, offering positive feedback of their experience, their encounters before and after that rail travel were not commensurate. Because so many people were arriving by bicycle, bikes were stacked nearly everywhere: sidewalks, railings, and filling up countless outdoor lots. The average person worried their bike would be damaged, stolen, or even lost in the endless sea of machines. Some Dutch cyclists even reported the practice of taking a picture of their bike and those surrounding it, in order to locate it at the end of the day—and that's if they found space in the racks at all, with many stations becoming home to thousands of orphan bikes. At Utrecht Centraal Station, an amazing 23 percent of bikes in their parking facilities have been abandoned, often by students leaving town and seeing more value in leaving their bike behind and purchasing another used one wherever they're heading to next.

"That was the reason for the Dutch railway and ProRail to begin investing in mobility," Miedema maintains. "Next to walking, bikes are one of the biggest modes for getting to and from the station. So for us, the bike is a very important mode to develop." Improving the quality of the bike-parking experience was the first step in achieving this goal. In 2000, NS worked in partnership with ProRail and the national government to begin a massive program to build a number of new parking facilities, both indoor and outdoor, with initial funding for 580,000 new spaces across the country. But, as has been noted in Utrecht, the initial predictions are already falling short of the stock needed to accommodate demand, and they are planning to add another 150,000 spaces nationwide in the coming years. The main challenge—as with any bike- or transit-related project around the globe—is budget.

"The problem," Miedema notes, "was from a big program developed in 1999, the government had already provided about €400 million [$494 million USD], and they wanted to end funding." In their own words, the national government said, "Let the local governments do it. We've done enough and we think it's a problem for local governments and Dutch railways." But NS, ProRail, and the local governments pushed back, pointing out that if funding stopped altogether, they would no longer be able to address the mounting difficulties. They noted that getting more people on bikes was actually solving many of the car-related issues affecting each station—largely around environmental impact and traffic. It was an easy sell. "We were able to get an agreement between all parties to start a new program over the next 15 years, with new solutions for the big problems we face," states Miedema proudly. "We want to innovate on the solutions we have. We want to search for how we can make it more profitable, and find how we can finance it together." And while there is still a €400-million shortfall for future projects, for now, they can keep moving on current initiatives.

NS and ProRail's more innovative work focuses on the various shelters they've built over the last 15 years, beginning with the question: How

Figure 8-2: Utrecht Centraal Station's spectacular 12,500-space bike-parking facility, which, when complete, will be the largest such structure in the world. (Credit: NS)

do you get people with less financial means—especially students—to use these facilities? "From the studies we did, we came up with a 'first 24 hours free' concept," explains Miedema. "Only people who stay in the shelter longer than 24 hours have to pay." Passengers check in with their OV-Chipkaart: a single smart card that provides access to the entire nationwide mobility system (train, tram, bus, OV-Fiets, etc.). It then tracks how long a bicycle is stationed in the lot, and, if more than 24 hours, charges a modest amount to the card. However, for smaller locations where paying for attendants was too expensive, they had to be more forward-thinking in their approach.

"We needed a new, user-friendly concept," Miedema concedes. To appeal to as wide a customer base as possible, they are rolling out a self-serve concept at 50 locations in the next few years, as well as a "fast-lane check-in" that aims to speed up the process during peak hours. The end goal is to reduce strain at stations, where they currently need several staff with handheld scanners to manage the sheer numbers entering and leaving the facilities during rush hours. Like the self-serve concept, the fast lanes are accessed via a secure gate opened by swiping the OV-Chipkaart, and the cyclist's account is charged right after checking out.

Undoubtedly, the most visible initiative in assisting the "last-mile" challenge is OV-Fiets, the rental scheme that provides passengers with a bike at their destination, for just €3.50 ($4.30 USD) per day. Started as a pilot program by NS, ProRail, and the government, the program has been growing in leaps and bounds each year, and as Lotte van Grol, product development manager with NS, explains, "OV-Fiets is really the 'last-mile' concept, and not a bike-share scheme, where you can pick up and drop off your bike at different places in the city. Primarily, we focus on the journey from the train station to the final destination and back to the station again. From our perspective, we are also a train operator; it is our goal to make the journey by train and public transport as fast, easy, and comfortable as possible. Furthermore, most Dutch people are really attached to their own bikes, so the people you reach with OV-Fiets, we presume, are not the people you reach with bike-share."

The success of OV-Fiets is also one of its greatest challenges. In 2010, the program boasted 800,000 rentals per year across 220 locations. Nowadays, that looks more like 3 million rentals per year across 310 locations, and—while that seems like a success story—supply meeting demand is an issue at some of the bigger train stations with limited space. For bikes arriving at the station, it is anticipated numbers will reach between 60 percent and 65 percent in the coming years. In order to accommodate such projected growth on that end of the journey, OV-Fiets would have to expand to 60 times its current size. "The biggest issue we have for OV-Fiets is that it is so successful, we don't have the space we need to park the bikes at the busier locations," confesses Van Grol. "There is simply not enough space to park more bicycles."

Despite the presumed shortage of rentals, residents are largely satisfied with the program. When surveying users, 89.6 percent of respondents gave OV-Fiets a 7-out-of-10 or higher. "It's high when you compare it to the Dutch railways itself," Van Grol points out. "People like to complain about the trains a lot. But when it comes to OV-Fiets, it's a positive thing we have." So positive, in fact, that Van Grol and Miedema are hosting an increasing number of international delegations seeking to learn about the Dutch bike–train model, particularly OV-Fiets.

While still not a perfect fix, NS and ProRail have recognized that to solve the "last-mile" problem they need to think creatively to provide an equitable, sustainable model that works for everyone. Coupled with the fact that NS recently made a 100 percent transition to renewable, wind-powered energy for their entire rail network, millions of Dutch residents now have access to a "green" carbon-free transportation solution—from the moment they step outside their front door to the moment they arrive safe and sound at their destination. Bringing the entire family along for the ride is made easier with the "Railrunner" fare, which allows children under the age of 11 to travel anywhere in the country for just €2.50 ($3.10 USD).

"The time is really here to get more attention on the fact that it's green," declares Van Grol emphatically. "Before, it was just that people were using a bike because that's what they do. Now you see the tendency that it's also sustainable. But still I doubt that people are using OV-Fiets primarily because it is green. I think the main reason people in the Netherlands use OV-Fiets is that it's a great concept for your "last-mile" journey: it's fast, flexible, healthy, and it gives you a sense of freedom in a city other than your hometown."

Replicating the Dutch BiTiBi Model

There's no doubt that the Dutch desire to promote bike–train intermodality over private car use is garnering a great deal of international attention. The growing number of organizations examining their system in further detail, in an attempt to reproduce it and address typical gaps and problem areas, is a clear demonstration of this awareness. Perhaps the most ambitious of these studies is the European BiTiBi ("Bike-Train-Bike") Project—funded by the

European Union's Intelligent Energy Programme and 10 partners in five different countries. Beginning in 2014, they launched four different pilot projects over a three-year period—in England, Italy, Spain, and Belgium—with the aim of decreasing car use by several million kilometers per year, as well as carbon emissions by several hundred tons.

Clotilde Imbert is a French urban planner and a partner at the Copenhagenize Design Company, who—despite the firm's Danish roots—acted as consultants on BiTiBi. She touts the Dutch model for a number of strategic advantages. The first, which Roland Kager also identified, is how the two complementary modes feed each other in a virtuous cycle, because both are scalable—unlike systems that allow bikes directly on public transit. "It's free of charge, and it works well in the Copenhagen area, for example, but it's definitely not for many cities," Imbert admits. "The new generation of urban trains are large, which makes it quite easy to fit bikes onto them. But that's not the case in many countries." Typically, the Copenhagen trains run under capacity, she notes, so officials are forced to find a way to fill it—in this case, an entire car dedicated to bicycles. "Most of the time, in most cities, the metropolitan trains are over capacity," Imbert explains. "You have too many passengers and too little space, with no room for bikes. So it's not something you can replicate in a lot of cities."

The second advantage offered by the Dutch approach is convenience, experienced through the comprehensive, end-of-trip amenities found at most train stations, including secure parking, retail and repair shops, and a variety of rental bikes (including a few pedelecs). "Having all of these facilities at the train station makes your trip very convenient," says Imbert. "Each time I travel, I know that when I arrive at the station, I will have a place to safely park my bicycle." Imbert has witnessed an evolution of the train station in recent years into a service hub that's no longer about just the train, but mobility in general. "Even if you are not a train passenger, you know the station is a place where you can find some information about cycling, where you can go and repair your bicycle," she points out.

Another important aspect is the principle of predictability, particularly when it comes to the arrival station. "What you have to understand is with the OV-Fiets system, it's a national rental service, which is an important distinction from citywide public bike-share systems, like in Paris, Vancouver, or London," Imbert explains. "The system works differently, and the same service is offered all over the country. This means that everywhere you go, when you arrive at a station, you know you can rent the same bicycle with the same card. You know how to get a bicycle, how the system works, and how much the service costs." This creates a significant advantage for users who don't want to wait for a bus, tram, or metro, and are unfamiliar with the local transit system. "And with only one card, you have access to the entire mobility system, including everything related to bicycles," she adds.

Figure 8-3: Operated by the national rail company, and available at 310 locations, OV-Fiets serves as the countrywide "last-mile" bicycle-rental system. (Credit: NS)

A 2011 user study found concrete evidence that these crucial elements of scalability, convenience, and predictability have directly influenced Dutch residents' travel decisions, with 8 percent of OV-Fiets users admitting that, without its existence, they would have driven a car door to door instead of using the rental service as part of a bike–train journey. Similarly, 54 percent reveal that they now use the train more often because of its availability, while 46 percent use it as an easy and healthy alternative to the bus or tram for the "last mile" of their trip.

Imbert also notes the increased efficiency of using bikes to feed transit, with a typical person moving five times faster on a bicycle than on foot, while expending virtually the same effort. At an average speed of 15 km/h (9.3 mph)—versus 3 km/h (under 2 mph) on foot—they can cycle 5 kilometers (3.1 miles) in the same time it would take to walk 1 kilometer (0.62 mile). By extrapolating those longer distances in every direction around a station, suddenly these efficiencies increase exponentially. This allows for larger station service areas, and fewer stops for the system. "The catchment area becomes 25 times bigger if the passengers cycle instead of walk," she explains. "Increasing it from just 3 square kilometers [about 1 square mile] to over 79 square kilometers [31 square miles] in size."

Of course, it should go without saying that these considerations are pointless without high-quality bike infrastructure leading directly to the transit stop, which cannot be located on an imaginary island surrounded by busy streets and unpleasant cycling conditions. "It sounds a little bit surprising, but in some countries you see train companies implementing new bicycle-parking facilities, but they don't talk to local stakeholders or authorities, and don't have proper infrastructure to reach the stations," Imbert explains. For her, it means taking the CROW design principles of cohesion, directness, safety, attractiveness, and comfort, and continuing to apply them through the door and onto the platform.

While it is still early in the pilot project process, BiTiBi's partners in Liverpool, Milan, Barcelona, and Ghent have seen some impressive results. For example, establishing secure bike-parking and rental schemes has resulted in fewer car trips, as 15–20 percent of bike-parking users who have stopped driving to the station, while 5 percent of rental-bike users left their cars at home. These pilot projects also managed to induce new cycling trips, with 40–50 percent of bike-parking users new to cycling, as were 70 percent of rental-bike users. This virtuous cycle also resulted in more train trips, with 20 percent of bike parking users new to train travel, as were 30–40 percent of rental bike users. Fewer cars, more cyclists, and more train passengers—an impressive return on a relatively modest investment in bicycle parking and rentals.

Imbert insists that, despite these preliminary achievements, the four pilot cities still have a long way to go, and mastering multimodality isn't as simple as sticking up some racks and filling them with rental bikes. "If I have one piece of advice, it's to make sure the train companies and transport agencies team up with the local authorities to design and build a comprehensive system, because we are really talking about a door-to-door approach," she suggests. "If there is one element missing, it means the system won't be as efficient as it should be. It could be the bicycle infrastructure; it could be the location of the parking relative to the station; it could be the card used to access these transport systems." Bringing teams of people together to shape a complete and inclusive system isn't easy, but it is vital for success. "If you develop only one part, it won't really work," she concludes.

While Copenhagenize Design Company's work is focused primarily on the European context, Imbert sees the bike–transit merger as one that could be acutely applicable to sprawling North American megacities. "In the Netherlands, we're talking about a national scale," she concedes. "But in North America, it can be very relevant at the scale of the metropolitan area." So relevant, in fact, that the least likely of locations are now integrating bikes and transit.

Combining Bikes and Transit in Sprawling Atlanta

In recent years, some North American urban planners have begun to explore ways to unlock Dutch-style multimodality, hoping to utilize the bicycle as a tool to increase public-transit ridership and decrease car dependency. In fact, the case could be made that—with the right conditions—bikes are better placed to deal with the lower population densities and longer distances traveled on their side of the Atlantic. Metropolitan Atlanta is perhaps the epitome of American auto-centric development: a vast region of 5.7 million people, where half of all trips are over 7 kilometers (4.5 miles) in length, and 95 percent of those journeys are made by private automobile. Transferring those trips to the bicycle alone is not a realistic expectation, so officials are looking at ways to combine cycling and transit in an attempt to improve access to employment, contribute to healthier lifestyles, reduce household costs, and increase the number of transportation options.

In 2014, the Atlanta Regional Commission (ARC)—the organization responsible for land-use planning and transportation across the sprawling region's 20 different counties, 81 cities, and 17 towns—identified what they saw as an opportunity for tremendous growth in the cycling's modal share. "One-third of the population lives within a five-minute bike ride of a transit stop, and about two-thirds work within a five-minute ride, but only 0.3 percent are biking to transit right now," reveals Kat Maines, planner in the Atlanta office of Alta Planning + Design. "So there's a real opportunity to capture those trips, and the ARC was interested in learning about the barriers that exist now, and how we can help get people past those barriers."

The resulting document, entitled *Bike to Ride: An Idea Book of Regional Strategies for Improving Bicycling Access to Transit*, was published by the ARC and Alta Planning in 2016. It identifies the key physical and psychological barriers that prevent more Atlantans from cycling to transit. Envisaged as a series of concepts that municipal governments can use to design, fund, implement, and evaluate their own projects, the plan outlines various ways the bike–transit relationship can be strengthened, by viewing the entire door-to-door experience through the eyes of the user. This includes providing direct, low-stress bikeways that deliver people of all ages and abilities directly to transit stops, as well as convenient, secure bicycle parking at bus stops, "park and ride" lots, and rail stations.

Just as Dutch stations have become service hubs that are about more than just trains, "Bike to Ride" reimagined high-ridership "park and ride" lots as gathering places and community assets. "We suggested secure parking areas and outlined a number of different formats, with either the transit agency or a private vendor taking care of the operation," Maines says. "We also saw

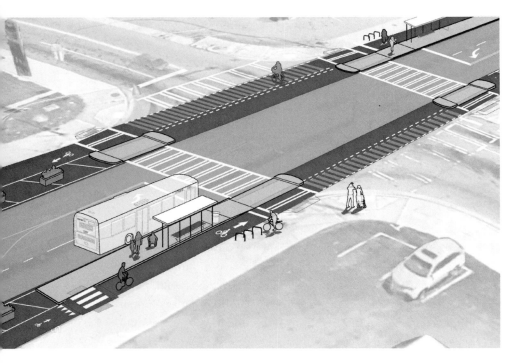

Figure 8-4: A design concept for a raised/floating bus stop, which incorporates bicycle parking and mitigates bike–bus conflicts. (Credit: Alta Planning + Design)

some examples where it was integrated with a bike shop or café, where you could drop off your bike and have it maintained during the day, as a way to establish the 'park and ride' not just as a place to get to, but as a place in and of itself." Atlanta already has a model for this, with the Metropolitan Atlanta Rapid Transit Authority's (MARTA) Transit-Oriented Development Program, whereby the agency sells all or a portion of its surface lots to developers for mixed-use developments sharing public space.

In a huge, diverse region with complications presented by a variety of urban, suburban, and rural settings, Maines has no illusions about which development pattern presents the biggest obstacle to their goal of growing active transportation: "I think the primary challenge is the suburban context. With local streets that end in cul-de-sacs on one end, and let out to busy

collectors or arterials on the other end, it's really hard to bike or walk to destinations," she laments. This lack of connectivity was a key problem identified in the plan, in response to which Maines and her colleagues proposed a
series of "cul-de-sac connectors" creating bike-priority arterials adjacent to
the main arterial roads.

Those lower-density areas bring with them another issue: a lack of per-
vasive, reliable public transportation. "Our stations, especially as you get farther out of the city, are very far apart," Maines explains. "So you could be
right next to a transit line, and not really be served by it." With vast numbers
commuting (mostly by car) from these suburban areas to four major "activity centers" in the region already served by public transit, the hope is that
cycling can be used to connect these neighborhoods to existing rail and bus
lines, and "feed" the system with larger catchment areas, much as the Dutch
understood years ago.

Encouraging suburban commuters to leave their cars in their driveways—
and thereby reducing the amount of traffic congestion—also means spending
more money on public transport, something a growing number of American
electorates appear to understand. In a move becoming reassuringly familiar in US cities paralysed by traffic, Metro Atlanta voters approved a half-
cent sales-tax increase in the October 2016 election, raising $2.5 billion for
MARTA over the next 40 years. These funds should go a long way to increase
the system's speed, frequency, and size, which—when complemented with
better biking facilities—will make public transit a more convenient choice
for far more residents.

A citywide bike-sharing scheme is another strategy that the City recently
implemented to provide residents, employees, and visitors with a first- and
last-mile solution, although its restricted service area limits it to three major
activity centers and the surrounding neighborhoods. Launched in June 2016,
Relay Bike Share began with just 100 bicycles at 10 docking stations, but
recently underwent a fivefold expansion, reaching into historically underserved areas. "With their second phase, their goal is to have bike-share at
every transit station in Atlanta," Maines discloses. "Transit and mobility are
big components of equity for the City. So they are trying to expand bike-
share outside more affluent parts of town, where it started." Relay officials

are also working to ensure that it is accessible to everyone, regardless of economic means: "They offer a reduced rate for low-income residents, which is five dollars a month. They also hire 'Atlanta Bike-Share Champions' from the Westside neighborhoods to lead education and outreach in those areas."

However, the "carrots" offered to incentivize more-efficient modes often neglect to include the "sticks" that disincentivize driving, beginning with the cost and availability of car parking, a strategy complicated by the City of Atlanta's decision to privatize its parking services. "Atlanta has had the same parking vendor since 2008, PARKatlanta, who got a really good deal with the City," Maines explains. "The way their contract was structured, PARKatlanta was incentivized to ticket, and not to increase their actual rates, because they were getting huge profits from the tickets, and not the meter rates." Maines believes that the new contract with ATLPlus signed in 2017 will bring with it much-needed change, including a more dynamic funding model, and rates that reflect the market price of precious storage space.

But those pricing increases won't affect the large number of private vendors offering parking for rather cheap. "The reality is we have a lot of surface parking in the city, and the way the tax code is set up right now, the owner pays based on what their land use is, not the highest value they could get," Maines points out. An upcoming rewrite of the City's development code has made her optimistic for a fix, but it won't instantly solve decades of systematic car-first policy and design. "The way it is right now, it's still pretty easy to drive into the city, unfortunately," she says. "And there's still a lot of 'park and ride' lots at transit stations, and a lot of people drive to them, and take transit the last three miles of their trip."

In addition to these physical barriers, there are a number of psychological ones that Maines and her colleagues encounter: "There's a bit of a stigma towards transit. It's becoming less and less, but historically a lot of suburban places didn't want transit in their neighborhoods because they thought it would bring the 'wrong kinds' of people," she says. There are reasons to believe the tide is turning, though. Recently, both Clayton and Gwinnett Counties passed resolutions to be included in MARTA. "So the transit agency has already expanded bus service into Clayton County to the south, and has plans to expand into Gwinnett in the north, and there are opportunities for other counties to buy in," she suggests optimistically.

Biking in particular is susceptible to these mental hurdles, particularly when it comes to being perceived as a mode of transportation rather than recreation, based on the people who are (or aren't) already pedaling on Atlanta's hostile streets. "There are a lot of people who might not have a stigma against bicycling but are nervous to do it, because they don't see others doing it generally," Maines submits. "Or the folks they do see out in the suburbs are riding a cheap mountain bike on a sidewalk to get to a bus station. And they don't see that as something that's desirable, something they want to be doing in their life. We want to create an environment where people driving may see someone using a well-designed bike lane, with separation from traffic and nice landscaping, and feel tempted to get out of the car and join them." This is where the region's larger walking and cycling plan—dubbed "Walk.Bike. Thrive!"—becomes critical, as an environment is shaped to entice the "interested, but concerned" crowd onto their bikes, thus attracting more casual riders, and engendering a culture where cycling is a perfectly normal and acceptable way of getting around.

In the two years since the "Walk.Bike.Thrive!" and supplemental "Bike to Ride" reports were published, the ARC has been quick to start implementing the programs and policies around it. "A lot of the local governments here are very low-capacity when it comes to active transportation, so it's about giving them the tools they need to create success on their own," Maines indicates. That includes a regional trails vision that closes priority gaps and identifies new trails of regional significance, hosting walk- and bike-friendly community workshops with cities and towns, completing a data-intensive analysis of high-crash-rate corridors via a Safety Action Plan, and building an online bicycle and pedestrian resource center. "This is a resource geared towards planners and public officials who may not have the training or capacity to hire a consultant for bicycle and pedestrian planning," she says.

As they race headfirst into the project-implementation phase, Maines is unequivocal that one factor will make or break the region's efforts to get more residents walking, cycling, and using public transportation: communication. "With 98 cities and towns involved, there's a lot of coordination that has to happen between them, and a lot of responsibility delegated to community or business improvement districts," she says. "There are a lot of different jurisdictions, and a lot of the time they just don't talk to one another. So there would be really good synergy that would occur if there were more conversation happening."

Despite the decades-long task ahead of them, everyone involved in Atlanta's "Bike to Ride" project is safe in the knowledge that, at the very least, they are all pushing in the same direction, a fact all the more astounding when you consider that they're working in an environment designed for and dominated by motor vehicles for over half a century. "The City of Atlanta's chief bicycle officer has told us, 'We're not adding capacity to any more roads. We're actually looking to take vehicle capacity away to increase person capacity on our streets,'" Maines reveals. "So they're not looking to accommodate any more cars in this city, but they are very focused on getting more people walking, biking, and using transit."

09 PUT YOUR CITY ON THE MAP

The Hovenring is a joy for thousands of commuters who now pedal into and out of Eindhoven every day — and an emphatic statement by a city that knows where it's going.

—*WIRED* MAGAZINE
"8 Cities That Show You What the Future Will Look Like"

As the home of Royal Philips Electronics for over 125 years, the southern city of Eindhoven—now the fifth largest in the Netherlands, with over a quarter-million residents—once epitomized the industrial heart of the country. During that period, its design, development, and economic vitality were inextricably linked to the electronics giant—long the city's largest employer, ever since the lightbulb factory opened its doors during the First World War.

Right after the war ended, recognizing the unprecedented growth a booming Philips would bring, Eindhoven hired nationally renowned architects Pierre Cuypers and Louis Kooken to develop a master plan for the region. Their inspiration—the "Garden City" imagined by British planner Ebenezer Howard—would prove to be a precursor for modernist thought. The five villages surrounding Eindhoven would be annexed and connected by a "ring road" intended solely for automobiles, while residential living would be pushed to suburbs outside of that perimeter. The interior would be for industry and shopping—a geographic separation of the three main functions of daily life: dwelling, business, and commerce.

"From the very beginning, the city was planned and designed for the car," suggests Bas Braakman, bicycle policy advisor for the City of Eindhoven. "That means the mindset of the inhabitants is still very much car-based. We face a bit more struggle than other cities, like Amsterdam and Utrecht, in making the transition to more sustainable modes of transport." But, as with many other locations across the country, it wasn't until after the Second World War that traffic engineers were handed the keys to shape the city in their ideal image.

"Eindhoven itself was bombed several times during the war—both by the Allies and the Germans—because it had industries close to the center, and was close to the Arnhem bridge depicted in the film *A Bridge Too Far*," recounts Frank Veraart, assistant professor at the Eindhoven University of Technology, and co-author of *Cycling Cities: The European Experience*. Unlike Rotterdam, most of its structures were left standing, but the attacks provided officials with the perfect cover to start making room for the automobile. "Every single building that was only slightly damaged was demolished to make more space for cars," claims Veraart. "All with the bigger view of getting more cars into the town."

The motor vehicle, as Veraart points out, was seen as a status symbol, an expression of luxury, and a way to stimulate economic activity in the central area: "They viewed the car as a vehicle of wealth. So if you welcomed cars into your town, drivers would stop and spend their money." For Eindhoven, this meant building a number of roads through the city center and setting aside vast spaces for customers to park while shopping and dining.

Meanwhile, in 1947, even as that status symbol grew in popularity across the region, people on bikes still constituted 71 percent of road users in Eindhoven (with motorists a mere 6 percent). But even in the face of that reality, American- and German-inspired professionals such as Dutch architect Jaap Bakema pursued their own form of social engineering, and any benefits to cyclists were either incidental or intended to get them out of the way of cars.

Vertical separation became one of the popular ways to get cyclists out of sight (and out of mind), as was the case of the Woenselse railroad crossing, a major bottleneck for the huge number of Philips employees biking between the factory and Woensel, a blue-collar neighborhood to the north. Often these gates would remain closed for five hours a day, causing massive delays for commuters. A solution wasn't implemented until 1953, when a tunnel was built to allow passage for cars, which proved equally beneficial to cyclists.

A brand-new train station was built three years later, but even still, decisions surrounding that were made with an eye on making it easier for motor vehicles to move freely throughout the city. "They elevated the railway tracks," explains Veraart. "That relieved traffic, so it could flow without hindrance. At that time, the whole idea was building the city for cars, rather than bicycles." This was in spite of the fact that, as late as the 1960s, 80 percent of all Philips employees (from factory workers to corporate executives) cycled to work daily.

Then, in 1961, the City hired German civil engineer Karl Schaechterle—a colleague and successor of M. E. Feuchtinger, the man who had proposed the calamitous demolition of Utrecht's medieval center five years earlier—to draw up a traffic plan to solve their ever-worsening congestion and road-safety problems. His idea, in its most basic form, was to prevent the "slow" traffic from obstructing the "fast" traffic, realized through dedicated bike paths and tunnels built adjacent to and underneath new car-only thoroughfares—wide, seamless boulevards that greatly expanded the capacity of the existing ring road as they radiated from the suburbs into the city center. One of the more interesting experiments in this vertical separation was the Berenkuil ("Bear Pit")—a sunken bicycle roundabout built in the early 1970s below the intersection of the perimeter ring road and one of those radial roads.

Eindhoven continued implementing both horizontal and vertical separation into the next decade, completing a 155-kilometer- (100-mile-) network of cycle paths and eight tunnels and bridges by 1976. Separating these transportation networks, however, was more about appeasing frustrated motorists than encouraging and enabling cyclists. "We were one of the cities in the Netherlands that were the quickest and most serious in doing that," claims Braakman. "But it was not meant to facilitate cycling at all. It was meant to facilitate car drivers." That meant the bicycle routes were often indirect and inconvenient, forcing cyclists to take uncomfortable and unnecessary detours, as was the case of the Berenkuil.

These efforts to prioritize driving had the intended effect, and Eindhoven's cycling modal share bottomed out in the late 1970s, accounting for just one in five trips. There it remained, until the city reached an unexpected and unwelcome watershed in the early 1990s, with Philips' decision to relocate its manufacturing offshore and its headquarters to Amsterdam. When their second-largest manufacturer, automotive company DAF, suddenly went bankrupt a year later, Eindhoven abruptly found itself in a grave economic and existential crisis.

Rebranding a Car Town into a Cycling City

"At that point, Eindhoven was statistically one of the poorest cities in the Netherlands," discloses Veraart. "And it even qualified for EU funding, like other southern European cities going through tough times." But rather than accept their fate, leaders opted to pivot away from industry and towards technology, attempting to attract new start-ups and revive their region as a "Silicon Valley of Europe." "With this flow of new energy," continues Veraart, "Eindhoven started to rebrand itself as a city of technology, design, and knowledge. As part of this rebranding process, it also wanted to rid itself of old views, like being a car town."

Veraart believes that the city's desire to put itself on the map was also driven by a form of local status anxiety. "Eindhoven is the fifth largest city in the Netherlands, but the four above it—Amsterdam, Rotterdam, The Hague, and Utrecht—are all in the northwest," he explains. "Eindhoven is the biggest outsider, so it needs an image of its own in the Dutch context." The city realized that reinventing itself would not be easy, but mobility could play a central role in that process. "They cannot undo the layout of the city, because that's engraved in stone, but they can at least try to picture themselves as being something different, and using the bicycle in this image building," offers Veraart. Central to that rebranding process has been the implementation of prestigious, headline-worthy bike infrastructure projects, useful for drawing international interest, such as the click-generating Hovenring, Eindhoven's now world-famous suspended bike roundabout, which opened in 2012 at a cost of €6.3 million ($7.8 million USD).

According to Braakman, the site selected for the Hovenring was definitely not arbitrary: "It was a major three-lane roundabout with no grade separation, a lot of congestion problems, and a lot of road-safety issues." That particular intersection was also located on a planned east–west cycling corridor linking the city center, the airport, and Veldhoven, home to the ASML campus: a Philips spinoff and the largest supplier of photolithography systems in the world. "In order to give right-of-way, and get more traffic through that intersection, we had to separate the networks of driving and cycling," says Braakman.

After considering numerous design options, including a series of Berenkuil-like sunken tunnels, the Dutch engineering firm ipv Delft presented the stunning circular suspension bridge concept, which took vertical separation to the next level. "It was more expensive," recalls Braakman, "but we saw it as an icon for Eindhoven." Fortunately, the politicians and decision makers involved saw tremendous value in investing in a symbol that sent a strong visual message home and abroad: "'This is how Eindhoven, like all the other Dutch cities, is paying attention to cycling,'" as Veraart puts it. "That's much easier than showing a map with the grid of cycle tracks, for example. That doesn't convey the message of 'We're working on it.'"

The overwhelming response to the Hovenring—a genuine shock to the humble Dutch—meant that shortly afterwards, when artist Daan Roosegaarde approached the City about his idea for a luminous bicycle path inspired by Vincent Van Gogh's beloved "Starry Night" painting, Braakman and his colleagues didn't hesitate for a second. "He was looking for a location near the village of Nuenen, where Van Gogh lived and worked for a number of years," he recollects. "One of our goals in Eindhoven is to facilitate all kinds of innovators. So we said, 'Okay, we have a bicycle path for you.'" Opened in 2014, the one-kilometer- (more than half-mile-) long trail combines solar-powered, glow-in-the-dark stones with LED lighting, creating a visual spectacle that recalls the region's pioneering past and bright future.

"That was a turning point for us," recounts Braakman. "We saw that, as policy makers, if you do something beautiful, something that has an impact on the image we have as a car-based city, we can use those examples to move towards more-sustainable modes of transport." He acknowledges that prestige projects are incredibly helpful in securing funding and attention from politicians, pointing to their warm reception by citizens and by people around the world. Cycling has become so normal in the Netherlands, and

Figure 9-1: The stunning "Starry Night" path, which allows visitors to cycle above and below the stars, combines glow-in-the-dark stones and LED lights. (Credit: Modacity)

the electorate so blithely accustomed to it, that these endeavors serve to get members of the public, media, and business community enthusiastic about bike infrastructure again: "I think for decades, we've taken the bicycle for granted. It is one of our strengths, but also one of our weaknesses."

With a newfound assurance that comes with executing such drastic and well-received projects, Eindhoven moved ahead in 2017 with its Groene Corridor ("Green Corridor") plan, the transformation of Oirschotsedijk, a collector road that moved 12,000 cars per day. "For us, that was revolutionary," says Braakman gleefully. "Everyone was shouting, 'You can't get rid of 12,000 cars!' But we did it anyway." What was once an arterial road that dissected Philips de Jonghpark, a private park owned by the Philips family, is now a delightful, family-friendly public green space, reconnected by a 5.5-meter- (18-foot-) wide bike path. "It is very successful," asserts Braakman. "It doesn't have the same impact as the iconic Hovenring. But in terms of the transition from car to bicycle, this may be even more radical."

Even before the Hovenring came along, Eindhoven was no stranger to making bold statements about its priorities and aspirations, as is evident with the 2009 transformation of 18 Septemberplein—the city's central public square. There, Italian architect Massimiliano Fuksas was hired to reclaim a place that had long been given over to cars—a former collector road and surface parking lot—into one for people: a vibrant gathering space and weekly market, with 1,500 underground bike-parking spaces accessed via two bicycle-friendly escalators covered by a pair of iconic, cone-shaped structures made of concrete and glass. When it was unveiled it received splashy illustrated coverage in both the *Washington Post* and *New York Times*, and now it serves exactly as intended, encouraging residents to visit the city center by bike (and spend money there).

Despite these pricey precedents, it's important to note that these kinds of high-profile ventures don't have to be costly, nor do they have to be so serious. One of Eindhoven's more recent projects takes advantage of its plentiful tunnels, as well as its status as an emerging design capital. As part of the City's new "Smile Factor" program, an initiative aimed at giving creatives a chance to work in their own city, graffiti artists Studio Giftig were commissioned to liven up the drab Dommel pedestrian and bicycle tunnel connecting the train station and university. The result: the "Silly Walk Tunnel"—130 meters (425 feet) of John Cleese's immortal *Monty Python's Flying Circus* sketch in which he depicted an official of the "Ministry of Silly Walks." A packed crowd attended the April 2016 unveiling, at which Cleese made a surprise appearance, remarking, "Do you seriously have nothing better to do today?" Reveals Braakman: "This was such a success that we have now 30 or 40 tunnels and underpasses, and a substantial amount of money available for artists to come up with their ideas."

In addition to drawing high-tech companies and talent from around the world, Eindhoven's new global, cycle-friendly image has another added

Figure 9-2: John Cleese's beloved "Ministry of Silly Walks" sketch is immortalized in a formerly drab bicycle tunnel as part of Eindhoven's "Smile Factor" program. (Credit: Modacity)

benefit: attracting tourists. "We currently have five million, which, within a couple of years, will be ten million passengers flying into Eindhoven Airport, and taking the first train to Amsterdam," explains Braakman. "One of our goals is to get them to stay in the city at least one night, and spend their money discovering Eindhoven. But that means you have to offer them something." For an increasing number of visitors, particularly young people, that something is a guided bike tour of the city, featuring the spectacular cycling infrastructure it has built over the years. "Our city marketing organization is doing really well," he says. "And it's becoming a lot more popular among city bloggers and weekend breakers."

With the completion of Strijp-S—an impressive, 27-hectare (67-acre) incubator lab and cultural hub housed within Philips' former manufacturing plants, Eindhoven has most certainly earned its new reputation as the Netherlands' "Brainport," complementing the country's two other points of entry. "Amsterdam is branded as a city of economics, partly because Schipol Airport is seen as the main economic driver of the region," Veraart points out. "Rotterdam is seen as the gateway to Europe, with one of the biggest ports on the continent. And Eindhoven now positions itself as being an innovative town, as a bright town. So it's now indeed attracting all types of industries, and presenting itself as a kind of 'Silicon Valley.'"

Carrying on this new spirit of invention are events such as the annual Dutch Design Week, which attracts over a quarter-million visitors and 2,500 designers to 100 locations across the city over a nine-day period in October. Similarly, since 2006 the annual GLOW Eindhoven Festival has invited local and world-renowned light artists to create colorful installations on dozens of building façades, interior spaces, and public squares across the city, which are offered as a self-guided walking tour for just one week.

Despite the positive gains, both Braakman and Veraart fear that this high-tech focus will bleed into the worlds of transport and planning, while overlooking the inherent spatial, social, and health benefits of the seemingly antiquated bicycle. "If you talk about Eindhoven, the university is very much pushing autonomous and electric vehicles as part of the sustainable-mobility solution. So it's pushing for four wheels instead of two," laments Veraart. Unlike Amsterdam and other fine-grained Dutch cities, the infrastructure and layout of Eindhoven are suited for both modes, offering few deterrents to the expansion of car use.

"That's the weakness of the bicycle: we see a lot of opportunities for smart mobility, but it's focused on car traffic," concurs Braakman, pointing to the Automotive Campus in nearby Helmond. There, entrepreneurs are doing all kinds of experimentation with the automobile, and are even using the motorway between the two cities as a testing ground for semi-autonomous driving. "So there's millions and millions involved in smart mobility solutions in the region, but only a small piece is invested in new technologies for bicycles," he states with frustration.

There is one field, though, in which Braakman hopes his city's car-friendly environment could provide a unique prospect for the right thinker. An excess of traffic lights makes for an exasperating amount of waiting time for cyclists, which could easily be reduced with a bit of high-tech tinkering. "There are a few new developments for cyclists using apps interacting with traffic lights, in order to get longer green times and shorter reds," he explains. "But these are only small experiments and pilots. I think there's a big opportunity to work with the CEOs of technology companies and make it not only about accidents and incidents, but to upscale it."

In the meantime, Braakman has his hands full advising Jannie Visscher, Eindhoven's deputy mayor for mobility, and hosting a rapidly growing number of international delegations through the Dutch Cycling Embassy. While these visitors always make a point of stopping in Amsterdam for a heavy dose of two-wheeled inspiration, they often depart Eindhoven—where cycling has since risen to a respectable 28 percent of all trips and 43 percent of all short trips—with much more practical ideas and motivation. "I hear a lot from those experts and decision makers that they actually think Eindhoven is more interesting for them, because it's more comparable," he says. "We have all this big infrastructure for car traffic, and all the barriers associated with it, and despite that we have a decent cycling mode share, and infrastructure like the Hovenring. Then they start realizing, 'Okay, so actually it is doable. It is feasible.'"

Bringing Beauty to "Oil Country"

Many North American cities have tried to reinvent themselves in recent years, with few as poignant as Detroit, which attempted to shed its "Motor City" reputation (despite being home to a number of bicycle manufacturers) after a 2013 bankruptcy and become a city known for innovation and creativity. North of the border, in Calgary, Alberta, a similar revolution is taking place. Most Canadians know Alberta as "Oil Country" due to its economic dependence on the oil-rich tar sands, and Calgary, Canada's third-largest city, is home to a number of oil and gas headquarters. Covering a 848-square-kilometer (327-square-mile) area—eight times the size of San Francisco—

and sprawling endlessly into the prairies, it's easy to see why driving has become the default mode of transportation for the vast majority of Calgarians.

In the past few years, however, things have started to shift, as residents have begun demanding options. At the heart of that transition sits Councillor Druh Farrell, who has proudly held her seat since 2001. It was during her tenure that Calgary's "Centre City Plan" was passed by a vote of the council under then-manager of city-center planning and design Brent Toderian, in which it was established that they would not consider any new river crossings for motor vehicles entering the downtown core. Situated where the Bow and Elbow Rivers meet, Calgary's downtown is accessible from the north and east only by means of a river crossing, resulting in several car-dedicated bridges that are largely unwelcoming to cyclists and pedestrians.

"The transportation system was fixed and we couldn't expand it any further," recalls Farrell of the May 2007 plan. "We needed to look at active modes and transit as bringing more people into our downtown core." The Centre City Plan identified three locations where potential bridges could be built, dictating two simple criteria: they had to be dedicated pedestrian and bicycle crossings only, and they had to be beautiful. But as Farrell soon found out, building something of beauty in "Cowtown" would not be as easy as it seemed.

"The Peace Bridge is red with my blood," she muses. All kidding aside, the Peace Bridge was the first of the three crossings to be built, and—at the time of construction—was one of the most controversial projects in Calgary's history. "For one thing, it was the first piece of significant infrastructure predominantly for active mobility," Farrell explains. "If it had been for vehicles, we would not have had any debate, and it would not have been controversial." Surprisingly, the issue wasn't solely with the intended users of the bridge. This was also the first time Calgary would make aesthetics a priority, engaging celebrated—and foreign—Spanish architect Santiago Calatrava to design the City's new bit of "bike bling."

Attractiveness aside, hiring Calatrava was about bringing in one of the most skilled bridge designers in the world in order to address some challenging site-specific concerns. The crossing, which would connect downtown Calgary to the northern river pathway and the community of

Sunnyside, had to completely span the Bow River, while also being flat enough to avoid obstructing the flight cone of a nearby helicopter-landing area. The practicality of bringing in the best-of-the-best didn't change people's opinions, however, and for the opening of the bridge, Farrell recalls having to be escorted by four bodyguards. "It was an incredibly painful process. It became so intense. The level of hatred directed towards that piece of infrastructure was out of proportion with the cost." The total budget for the bridge was $24.5 million (CAD), half the cost of a planned highway interchange in nearby Cochrane—18 kilometers (11 miles) west of Calgary—that would serve one-fiftieth of Calgary's population.

Farrell recounts that even her brother had to endure the ire directed at the Peace Bridge when a dinner guest discovered their relation and said to him, "You tell your sister that if we wanted beauty, we'd travel to Paris. In Calgary we just need it to work." Despite that prevailing attitude—that Calgarians come to the city solely to make their fortune, and then travel elsewhere to experience vitality and beauty—she stood firm, defending the city council's decision. "Now I think most Calgarians would recognize it was worth it," she asserts emphatically. "I certainly believe it was worth it because the bridge is so well used."

Since its ribbon-cutting on March 24, 2012, the Peace Bridge has become one of the most-traveled walking and cycling routes in the city, boasting over 5.5 million crossings, an average of 28,000 per week—not bad for a region that enjoys a meagre 1.75 percent modal share for cycling. Farrell notes that in spite of the initial negativity directed towards the undertaking, it stands out as a memorable pivot point for Calgary. "The Peace Bridge really was a first for a lot of reasons," she says. "It got people talking about architecture, and it identified a bottled-up need and desire for more walking and cycling connections to our downtown core." In the years to follow, the City constructed the George C. King and Elbow River Traverse bridges—a pair of pedestrian and cycling connections to the east of downtown, with a fourth crossing planned to the west when demand grows to sufficient levels.

The iconic structure has become more than just a gateway to the city. "What we ended up doing unintentionally with the Peace Bridge is building

Figure 9-3: As Calgary's first piece of infrastructure for active mobility, the Peace Bridge was also the first time the City prioritized beauty. (Credit: City of Calgary)

a public space over the river," recalls Farrell. "It's far more than a transportation hub or connection—it's a meeting place, a sense of place, on top of our beautiful river. It's the most photographed structure in the city. It's used for the promotion of Calgary in everything from real estate to hotels, and included in international bridge-design showcase books. It reinforces that we did the right thing."

"The Peace Bridge was a turning point for Calgary," she adds. "It symbolized that we are building a great city, that we want people to fall in love with their city, and that we deserve better. It presented competing visions of what Calgary was all about." In fact, the Peace Bridge laid the groundwork for Calgary's next big cycling-infrastructure project, and Farrell's next political challenge: a downtown cycle-track network.

Within a year of the Peace Bridge opening, latent demand presented itself. As more people were using the trails and bridges to enter the city, it became abundantly clear they needed a comfortable place to travel once bursting onto the downtown streets. Farrell stood at the forefront, providing the initial push for the 7th Street cycle track that would connect directly to the Peace Bridge. Perhaps unsurprisingly, talk of reallocating road space spurred the usual anger, and even Bike Calgary—the local bicycle-advocacy group—were cautious about how a two-way cycle track would work, rather than painted one-way bike lanes.

"I insisted it had to be a separated cycle track," emphasizes Farrell. "It's going to be downtown, it has to be separated." After the construction of the 7th Street cycle track in 2013—a 750-meter (2,500-foot) bidirectional, curb-protected lane that quadrupled cycling numbers along that corridor overnight—talk began of a "minimum grid" to service the entire city center. Initially the project was to be completed in increments, much like Vancouver's AAA network, but the discussion suddenly shifted to the idea of building the whole scheme at once as an 18-month pilot project. It seemed to be smooth sailing ahead, with Bike Calgary coming around to show its support, when a change of council in 2013 made the politics more challenging.

As with the Peace Bridge, hostility towards the project from businesses and politicians was disproportionate to the cost of the project—$5.75 million—but what stood out for Farrell was the opponents' refusal to see it as an opportunity. Due to the pilot nature of the project, it meant that the system wasn't permanent, and the proposal narrowly passed by an 8–7 vote in April 2014. Then, on June 18, 2015, Calgary's downtown cycle-track network was delivered two months early and $2 million under budget, reallocating just 2 percent of the downtown street space to induce 1.2 million bicycle trips over 18 months, with little to no driver disruption.

"Pilots are so important. For one thing, we were constantly adjusting," explains Farrell, referring to the 100 tweaks that staff made in response to data collected at 80 different points. These changes were facilitated by the provisional nature of the scheme, including flexible delineators, planter boxes, temporary concrete curbs, and floating traffic signals. "The transportation department was extremely nimble in identifying problems and mitigating them. By the end of the pilot, the system worked. So they weren't just waiting until the end of the project to make adjustments—they were doing it all along and measuring the data. We had such a compelling case. We had more people cycling: different people, young people, women, and families were all using the network. It was hard to say 'no.'"

In December 2016, council voted 10–4 in favor of making the network permanent, meaning that the pilot had accomplished exactly what was intended: demonstrating to a skeptical public that—with safe, separated space for cycling—even the sprawling, frigid cities of the Canadian Prairies will get on their bikes. Councillor Diane Colley-Urquhart, who had initially voted against the pilot, decided to change her vote, telling reporters: "I was a person that didn't support this in the beginning. I thought this was madness. But, to see how it's evolved, and how it's working and to see how people are starting to get the fact that this is shared public space . . ." Best of all, Calgary created a template for others to copy, inspiring its peers in Victoria, Edmonton, and Winnipeg to plan their own cycle-track networks in the coming years.

Calgary's pilot is a persuasive example of how temporary installations can change hearts and minds, but most notably, it is now cited as a reason companies and talent are relocating to the city. After a downturn in the local economy due to the deflated price of oil, and a downtown vacancy rate hovering between 25 and 30 percent, continued investments in walking, cycling, public transit, and infrastructure such as the Peace Bridge will be integral in attracting new economies to this sprawling city. As Farrell points out, "If we want to attract new industries to Calgary, we need to first build a city that's worth moving to."

While her illustrious career is by no means at an end—she was elected to a sixth term in 2017—when Farrell reflects on her time on council, she is proud of how far her city has come. The old guard who stood in the way of progress is making way for a younger generation of politicians and entrepreneurs investing in innovation, and time is on their side. As a subtle reminder of her struggles, she made a small but important gesture to future generations: "When we did a time capsule for the new Bow Tower, I put in a drawing of the Peace Bridge with a letter to the future council 100 years from now that said: 'When investing in the city and in beauty, what will you remember—the controversy or the legacy?'"

The Practicality of "Velotopia"

Cities such as Calgary and Eindhoven have clearly seen value in branding themselves as imaginative and innovative places, and—even more so in the case of the latter—these investments have raised them from relative obscurity and put them in the spotlight for all the world to marvel over. The Hovenring and the Peace Bridge have served as catalysts, attracting people to visit, and even live in, regions that recognize the importance of not just making it easier to move about the city, but also making those trips visually stimulating. Equally important, however, are the practical solutions that extend beyond those iconic projects, helping cities to better handle the future transportation stresses that will inevitably arise as our planet's population continues to migrate from rural to urban settings.

Dr. Steven Fleming has held academic positions at the Universities of Tasmania and Newcastle in Australia, and Harvard and Columbia in the United States, and is also the director of Cycle-Space International, a consulting firm. A passionate voice in urban planning and cycling circles, he points out that while prestige projects can shine a spotlight on cities, they serve a much more meaningful purpose. In his 2017 book *Velotopia*, Fleming admits that flashy architecture and smart urban design are great, but there are many more practical reasons to build the cycling city.

"We can talk about cycling being red paint, and being deliberately shocking and creating icons and branding, but that's all take-it-or-leave-it stuff," he argues. "You could build anything to achieve that." Fleming identifies the danger with iconic design is that "starchitects" can't keep repeating the same trick. Frank Gehry can't build a Guggenheim Bilbao in every city and have the same effect. "So the purpose of *Velotopia* was to say, 'Hang on, there's actually a practical benefit here and that's to increase connectivity in the city.'"

Fleming looks for a tipping point in every region—the point when they can no longer build their way to better motorized connections. Once the population in any area reaches 5 million people—considered the economically important category where more wealth and opportunities are realized—they become "slow cities." By investing in cycling, governments can set themselves up better for the future. It's a common sentiment in every growing metropolis: they simply cannot accommodate any more vehicles in their centers and still enjoy a meaningful quality of life. So how do you maintain and improve connectivity for other modes that will put less strain on the existing system? By building bikes into the equation.

Fleming does warn, however, that placing too much value on prestige projects, or "bike bling," can distract from what is more important—the fact that a connection is a connection, and how it looks is irrelevant to how it functions. In June 2017, Fleming curated the world's first Bicycle Architectural Biennale in Amsterdam during the Velo-city Conference, but he resisted focusing on bicycle-specific infrastructure. "Infrastructure is just like a plumbing project," he claims. "It wouldn't exist if there wasn't a tap on one end and a dam at the other. I was more interested in the dams and the taps—what sort of building type acts like a tap—the starting point—and which types of buildings act as destinations for bike trips—where you want to head? Each of the buildings, in their own way, tells a kind of story for many cities."

Practicality aside, Fleming concedes that if good design creates pride in a place, then that can only be a good thing. In Bogotá, he is helping design a school and innovation center in an area that experiences a high rate of crime. They know that, culturally, good architecture inherently causes people to behave better, and a high value has been placed on ensuring beautiful design. He cites a view of architectural theorist Mark Wigley, a professor at Columbia University, that architecture is one's outermost layer of clothing. A person dressed down in jeans and a sweater might get away with cursing, but the same person dressed in a suit would have to behave very differently. "Similarly," Fleming contends, "the built environment dictates our behavior. People will love and care for beautiful architecture and will be proud of it and take care of it."

If anything can be taken from examples like the Hovenring in Eindhoven or even the Dafne Schippersbrug in Utrecht, it's the value of good design— which is to say, not design for design's sake, but functional design that serves a purpose beyond simply being attractive. The Dutch seem to have a special genius for this. "Some people attribute it to building the polders," Fleming explains, "but the Dutch talk to each other when they're designing things. It was only by the city and the school talking to each other that they were able to come up with the bridge on the school." Of course, a deep-rooted dedication to artistic literacy has helped train several generations of Dutch designers to think innovatively and a little bit differently. "There's a kind of knowledge that they don't have a lot of resources," Fleming suggests, "so they know they have to be innovative. They don't want to copy anybody; they want to do something no one has done before, so as soon as the design process starts, off they go breaking rules and venturing into new territory."

Cities around the world are in the midst of using the bicycle as that "red paint": an edgy branding tool for attracting newcomers and giving residents

Figure 9-4: Eindhoven's now-famous overpass for cyclists, the Hovenring, has become a symbol for a city that embraces the future and the value of functional, innovative design. (Credit: Modacity)

pride of place. Such is the case for projects like the Peace Bridge, the "Pink Lightpath" in Auckland, or the Bicycle Skyway in Xiamen, China—projects that have put cities formerly unknown for cycling onto the global map. And while these developments definitely stand out, the real importance still needs to be placed on creating attractive cycling spaces, not just icons.

Fleming points out that while cycling can appear to be flourishing to those "within the bubble"—cycling enthusiasts, urbanists, city builders—there are swaths of the population being underrepresented. Even the Netherlands, a country that enjoys the highest rates of cycling on the Earth, runs the risk of seeing those numbers drop as the baby-boomer generation is removed from the equation. Despite massive investments in cycling infrastructure every-where, such investments often mean little to immigrant populations, who tend to live farther outside of city centers and experience higher rates of bike theft due to a lack of quality bike storage—if they even have bikes at all. "It's hard to build up the cycling culture or interest in cycling without addressing these concerns first," Fleming indicates.

Projects like the Dafne Schippersbrug and Amsterdam's Nescio Bridge help address these real and immediate issues. Whereas the former provides residents of the sleek new Leidsche Rijn neighborhood with a direct link to Utrecht and the central station, the latter connects less-affluent areas of Amsterdam to the city center. In both cases, the bike connection is more effi-cient than the car and rail links, fundamentally increasing accessibility to cycling in those outer boroughs.

"This is the nice thing about Dutch design—they have cycling not just in their city centers but everywhere," says Fleming. "So it's in the Dutch brain to pick one street and say this is a street for bikes and another is a street for cars." Fleming notes that, when identifying possible new bicycle routes, it's not about having all modes of transportation share the same corridor, as is often prescribed on North American streets. The focus is more on what makes the most sense for that given space, with simple solutions favored wherever applicable. "It's all about decoupling cycling, and when you have that decoupling mindset, it becomes quite natural to say, 'Here's an area that has a lot of cyclists and here's an area that has a lot of cars, and they're each quite happy to have their own space.'"

As for the role prestige projects will play in the future of our cities, Fleming is skeptical. "Where do you go with shocking, brilliant architecture? As with the art world, you get to a certain point where there's nowhere further to go. It's a meta-narrative that architecture will continue to get more shocking and brilliant until you end up with Jackson Pollock. And then it gets to 'Now what?'" More important than creating beautifully designed infrastructure, Fleming emphasizes, is recognizing that all this becomes moot when air pollution, congestion, and traffic fatalities—all major externalities of the private automobile—lead to car-free cities. Enabling people to maintain safe, reliable connections without depending on cars is the most viable, practical way forward—even in Velotopia.

10 LEARN TO RIDE LIKE THE DUTCH

The Dutch have created the safest and most complete bicycling network in the world, but we need to look beyond infrastructure and into their collective souls to better understand why riding a bicycle is so normal in the Netherlands.

— CHARLES RUBENACKER
Dutch and American Cycling Spokesman, Rubenacker and Company

Beyond the paint, planning, and policies, what has nurtured the bicycle's supremacy in the Netherlands—despite a minor blip in the 1970s—is that cycling has been a part of their social fabric for over a century. To the Dutch, as Carlton Reid points out, riding a bike is just a normal part of the everyday for virtually everybody. The challenge for coming generations will be to maintain that level of normalcy as the nation experiences a convergence of socioeconomic factors, including a disturbing trend towards *de achterbank-generatie* ("the backseat generation") and a sharp rise in cultural diversity.

Since the 1970s, Dutch cities have been experiencing consistent growth in their immigrant populations, people from southern Europe and Turkey, as well as Morocco and other North African countries, either immigrating with their families or seeking refugee status. Often, increases in "non-Dutch" populations are blamed for low ridership numbers, with politicians and policy makers stating that immigration "dampens the levels of cycling growth." To Angela van der Kloof, a researcher for Mobycon, a Dutch sustainable-mobility consultancy, this attitude is both inaccurate and counterproductive.

Van der Kloof has been teaching biking skills to migrant groups for over 25 years and is a frequent speaker on the topic of growing cycling in immigrant communities. When people point to a perceived difference in cultural values to explain reduced cycling rates, she begs to differ. "We're all humans," she states. "We all have mobility needs. Between 'native' Dutch people there are a lot of differences, just as there are a lot of differences between newcomers. But there are likely more commonalities. This whole discussion in the cycling field, of putting a stamp on people's foreheads, saying, 'You're a non-native, you cycle less than the Dutch'—I don't like it. I'd rather look at longer-term perspectives."

While exact data is difficult to find, first- and second-generation migrants make about 20 percent of their trips by bike, a rate almost every global city would love to see. But because they don't cycle at the same levels as their Dutch peers, it becomes easy to frame ethnicity negatively. Van der Kloof feels it's a telling indicator of what the Dutch take for granted every day: that cycling is so ingrained in their society. Few ever consider the fact that immigrants may come from cultures where riding a bike just isn't done, even in "developed" countries such as the United States, Canada, Australia, or New Zealand. Not to mention that for many women, there often still exists a taboo around cycling that many Westerners would not understand. But it's the commonalities she has come to appreciate—particularly the shared desire for the freedom to move and be in control of one's independence. "The fact that you're a Muslim," she insists, "doesn't say anything about your transportation habits or choices."

Van der Kloof began teaching migrant women how to ride in 1991, after she stumbled on a classified ad for trainers at the Immigrant Women's Center in her community. As a master's student of human geography, studying women in North Africa and the Middle East, she had done a great deal of reading on the topic, but wanted to do something more meaningful. "It was never my plan, but the beautiful thing about these initiatives I've seen over the years is that the need or request for these services comes from the people who want to learn," she explains. "That's the reason I've stuck with it for such a long time: it is really a bottom-up, grassroots program, and that's its main strength. People *want* to learn to ride bikes."

Figure 10-1: For many immigrant women in the Netherlands, the bicycle quickly provides a newfound freedom and independence. (Credit: Modacity)

Soon after these women arrived in the Netherlands from elsewhere, they began to attend courses to learn the language and skills needed to adapt to their new life, and they often asked if there were programs available to show them how to ride a bike. Immediately recognizing that they were living in a nation of bikes, they clearly saw that they needed cycling proficiency in order to gain for themselves the freedom to move around their new surroundings easily. "These programs don't start because somebody in government says, 'Hmm, this makes sense to teach people to ride bikes, because it's part of our mobility system,'" Van der Kloof clarifies. "It is only now we are starting to realize that if you cannot cycle, you suffer from 'transport poverty.'"

Common in low-income and migrant areas in the Netherlands, transport poverty defines places with limited mobility options, whether public transport, cycling, or otherwise. In Rotterdam, for example, research indicates un- and under-employed residents south of the River Maas don't have access to the same economic opportunities enjoyed by people elsewhere in the Netherlands, in part because of how the transport system works. Van der Kloof notes that addressing cycling is one part of alleviating transport poverty. It is also why they bring these courses directly to the people. "The women participating in these programs already have mobility problems," she emphasizes. "So it's silly to make them come to you. Our strategy is to go to them so they can learn. And once they can cycle, they can come to our activities at the main center."

Van der Kloof has noticed that in many of the areas where she's worked, word of mouth has been central to their success. "Once you have the first pioneers, and you have a good relationship with them, in a few weeks you might go from three to nine women. A few weeks later, there are twenty." But she stresses that, ideally, the groups should remain small, because it helps the women know they aren't the only ones struggling to learn to ride. It also helps them get to know their neighbors. "The whole experience is not just the trainer passing on knowledge to the group," she explains. "There is also an exchange going on amongst participants, not only about cycling, but it is also about life here in the Netherlands, and this shared experience."

Part of that shared experience, and something Van der Kloof maintains is vital to the program, is learning to negotiate real-life conditions. She recalls seeing similar schemes where participants learn to ride in a park, building the skills to use a bicycle but not necessarily apply these skills to their daily life. "It may make sense in cities where the built environment is not so great," she says. "But over here, why would you only teach people to ride circles in a park, when you want them to use it in their daily life?" In fact, she relishes the moments when she passes by former students on the street, using a bike to get from home to school, or the shop, or any other practical location, because it means they are enjoying the incomparable freedom and independence that cycling can offer.

"Sometimes people ask me if I did any before or after surveys," Van der Kloof recalls, "and we did think about it at the time, but actually, because we saw the women who had been participating out in the community, we didn't feel the need to register that or to put a lot of effort into surveying them. We saw what was happening. We saw the positive impact and listened when these women told us how it had changed their ability to move in their city."

Although she stopped teaching in 2008, Van der Kloof dedicates her free time to passing on her knowledge to those looking to bring similar courses to their own jurisdictions. In 1996, while partnering with Snjezana Matijevic, the director of the Center for Immigrant Women, to locate funding, she teamed up with volunteers and participants to develop training materials that focused on traffic rules, including a booklet still used today. She also trains other instructors, produces videos explaining her methods, and presents at conferences. As she points out, it doesn't have to be fancy, and often a simple guide with clear illustrations—for those still learning the language—goes a long way to help them learn the basics.

The greatest challenge in going forward with plans like these, she notes, is finding funding. Which political party is in control dictates financial priorities, and with a more conservative government, these types of programs are the first to be cut. As she points out, such budget cuts can have lasting effects: "It damages this whole network of people who have been trained, and have been enthusiastic to train others." But the effects don't stop with the trainers: "Once you have the women on the bikes, they manage to also get their men on the bikes, they can teach their children, they can go out together, they encourage their friends to do the same." The passing along of that knowledge from one group to the next has far greater impacts than just knowing how to ride a bike. She also points out that North American fundraising models are such that incorporating public and private donors is far easier, and could make such schemes simpler to fund and grow.

It is the cultural exchange that Van der Kloof feels makes the program so valuable: "I really believe in this way of doing things because it is so basic. I mean it's not rocket science. You have to do it bottom-up and you have to do it with your heart. Teaching skills is easy. Working on self-confidence and self-esteem, getting them to the point where they say, 'Okay, I am a person who can do this, I can imagine myself cycling in a street'—that kind of process is the hard part. You don't have to be an 'avid cyclist' to capture that and exchange it." She contemplates that sometimes being overly enthusiastic presents a disadvantage, because it can create a blind spot, making it hard to believe that riding a bicycle is difficult to do.

Reflecting on all those years of teaching, Van der Kloof shares this wonderful anecdote of what teaching immigrant women has meant to her: "With kids, you watch them grow and learn, until they reach this magic moment where you can take the training wheels off and watch them become independent. But when you teach an adult, you're not holding them but guiding them. It's like flying! It's a moment a lot of adults cherish and love to share with each other."

Practical Skills for the Next Generation

Given the obvious way that cycling seems to be a part of the Dutch DNA, one couldn't be faulted for thinking that Dutch kids must be born on a bicycle. Of course, the reality is that, just like all children across the globe, they experience the same stumbles and falls when learning how to balance on their own two wheels, until one day the moment comes when they no longer need their mother and father to hold them, and they learn to fly.

What makes the Netherlands stand apart from other countries, however, is the Dutch dedication to nationwide bike education for children. Jonneke Reichert is the program coordinator for traffic and health at the Fietsersbond, where she's actively involved in coordinating their cycling instruction programs. Their mandate: to empower more people to cycle more often. Having previously worked in the Ministry of Health, Welfare, and Sport, with a focus on prevention, Reichert sees the direct link between regular cycling and better health. "For us it's so normal," she says. "It's in our culture to start cycling at an early age. I think it's one of the things we don't think about much because it's so common." Reichert recalls her two-and-a-half-year-old daughter coming home from daycare with a diploma for Traffic Safety Learning, and not being surprised that she was learning these lessons at such a young age. For many regions, it is rather common for kids to navigate traffic lights, stop signs, and other conditions on "run bikes" (pedal-less bikes that toddlers use to get accustomed to balancing on two wheels) in a controlled course on the grounds of their preschool.

But their existence throughout the country does not mean that the value of these courses should be taken for granted. As Van der Kloof notes, in a nation where everyone bikes, learning to ride independently is a critical skill. "That's why we push it: because once they get older, we want them to cycle to school," Reichert affirms. "In the Netherlands, the distances are not that far from home to school, so it's one of the most important modes of transport. We try to get not only the children, but also their parents aware that it's a way for them to become independent at a young age, so it prepares them for when they grow up."

Once kids are of school age, cycling education normally becomes a part of their curriculum, and while this isn't compulsory across the nation, it is uncommon to find an institution that doesn't offer such training in some

Figure 10-2: A common sight on Dutch streets: children as young as five, who begin their training in preschool, cycling without adult supervision. (Credit: Modacity)

form. "Of course, we at the Fietsersbond want it to be mandatory," Reichert muses. For most Dutch children, their learning comes to a head around the age of 11, when they take a theoretical exam about traffic rules and safety. Reichert feels the more important exam, however, is the practical portion, where the kids pedal a selected route through their city, performing all the skills they've acquired in a real-life setting.

"Most people remember when they were 10 to 12, taking that test, where you would have a whole tour around the city where you live, with parent volunteers at various checkpoints in disguise to see how the children are doing. I remember cycling it with my father," Reichert reminisces. "You would always do it by yourself ahead of time, because you don't want to fail the test. So it's basically a part of growing up in the Netherlands." Approximately 200,000 kids participate in the program annually, and after successfully completing the exam, each is given a personalized diploma, something they can proudly display, knowing they're all set for the independence that riding a bike will bring.

Reichert, like Van der Kloof, argues that the situations presented in the practical exam are the most important part of the program. They do have some lessons in spaces where road conditions are simulated, with most schools participating in an education day at a dedicated "traffic garden." But once they've passed, students know what to expect when they start riding on their own, and parents are confident enough in their abilities to let them roam freely.

It sometimes seems that because of the success of this curriculum, most people in the Netherlands tend to take it for granted. This makes it difficult for the Fietsersbond to push for increased funding to get more people on bikes, because if the public perceives that it's so common, why is training even necessary? Reichert concedes that not enough Dutch people know what the Fietsersbond actually does, and so they have to get better at claiming the little victories.

That includes the rollout of their Traffic and Health Program in 2018. "It's too narrow to look only at traffic safety and how to improve it," she explains. "We believe that the more people you have cycling more often, the safer it gets. But it's also really important from a health perspective." She points out that the average trip to school is an easy way for students to get the recommended minimum 30 minutes of physical activity a day, as suggested by the National Health Advisory Board. Through her experiences in both the Ministry of Health and the Fietsersbond, Reichert has seen that there are some gaps to be bridged between the urban-planning world and the public health world. "The idea is that we try to connect them at the Fietsersbond. So when we talk about traffic safety, we look at the bigger picture: the more people who cycle, the safer it gets, and therefore the healthier people are."

This includes raising awareness in adults about how crucial they are to a cycling-friendly environment. By working with their local divisions, the Fietsersbond has developed maps identifying "safe drop-off" or "kiss-and-go" zones: areas where parents are encouraged to drop off their children and allow them to walk or cycle the final distance on their own.

Reichert is also quick to advise that while most Dutch kids complete their practical cycling exam by 12, the Fietsersbond's work with these kids does not end then and there. They continue their work into high school, emphasizing that it's not only about learning how to cycle, but also how to behave in traffic, with a focus on behaviors more common in teens.

Looking ahead, Reichert says that in the coming years there will be a focus on directing their marketing to young people, with a campaign highlighting the Fietsersbond's education programs and teaching them about the inherent health benefits connected to cycling. She also notes that it is high time the Dutch start celebrating what a remarkable cycling culture they have. "I think it's important to showcase that what we have is quite special. It's been repeatedly pointed out to us, and we want to commemorate in some way," she explains. The first idea on the list: lobbying UNESCO to get cycling identified as a key element of the Netherlands' national identity, because it is something the Fietsersbond and many other Dutch people are—or at least should be—incredibly proud of.

Reaching Seattle's Next Generation of Riders

As more and more North American cities begin investing in budding networks of cycling infrastructure intended for all ages and abilities, the conversation has shifted to how leaders, advocates, and community organizers can complement their efforts with education and outreach programs aimed at the next generation of riders. Finding a realistic and relaxed environment in between the classroom and the real world can be a significant challenge, but is absolutely essential for getting people who are hesitant about cycling to give it a try.

Steve Durrant—a Seattle-based landscape architect and vice president of Alta Planning + Design—was visiting Copenhagen in 2014 when he encountered just such a safe space: one of their bustling *Trafiklegepladsen* ("traffic playgrounds"), complete with painted streets, roundabouts, traffic lights, road signs, and pedestrian crosswalks. "It was in the fall, and it was a crappy weekend day, and I was thinking, 'Well great, I'm not going to be able to see anyone actually using it,'" he recalls vividly. "But it was full. There were all sorts of kids and families in there, really tiny kids, and it was really inspiring to see."

As a certified instructor for the League of American Bicyclists, Durrant immediately recognized the power of such an immersive and experiential teaching space. "Usually what happens is that we find a parking lot, take tennis balls or traffic cones, mark out a route, and say, 'Imagine this is a street,'" he explains, admitting that most students have difficultly visualizing a few parking stalls as a real-life street. "Especially for kids," he acknowledges. "Just watching them attempt to make use of a space like that is really complicated."

Upon returning to Seattle, Durrant didn't have to wait long for an opportunity to channel this newfound inspiration and build what might be North America's first "traffic garden." While working on the site design for a new Northeast Seattle headquarters for Cascade Bicycle Club, one of the nation's largest bike clubs, he proposed that one be built in an adjacent alleyway, which opened in the spring of 2016 as a teaching space for their educational programs. While it wasn't nearly the scale and scope he would have hoped, it did lay the groundwork for a larger, more extensive project in a south Seattle park a few months later.

One of Cascade Bicycle Club's more virtuous and fruitful programs is the Major Taylor Project (MTP), an after-school program that hopes to empower youth from diverse communities through bicycling. "They had been approached by King County Parks about a little-used park in a neighborhood just south of Seattle, in White Center, and wanted to activate part of it," explains Durrant, who suddenly found himself with the blank canvas of two tennis courts that had been made obsolete by the opening of a new tennis center nearby. "There were two foundations [the YES! Foundation and the White Center Community Development Association] that had money ready to get into a community-building project like this," he says. "And Cascade Bike Club was ready to provide the services. So we just rolled into it."

Providing his professional services in exchange for promotional consideration during the Cascade Bicycle Club's varied annual events, Durrant transformed those two abandoned tennis courts into a functioning miniature streetscape, intended to help kids learn the skills necessary to operate a bicycle and become familiar with roadway marking and signage. From the day the "traffic garden" opened, Durrant could see how quickly kids picked up on the intuitive design: "They just understood it. They didn't need any orientation to what they were looking at. Stick to the right. Stay on the road. Stop at the crosswalks. It was pretty cool."

With the addition of a reclaimed shipping container to serve as an ad hoc storage and maintenance area, the White Center Traffic Garden has also served as a home base for local MTP participants. "A big part of what they're doing there is trying to provide activities that help kids realize their potential as leaders," describes Durrant. "They're looking to improve opportunities for people of color, people of lower income, and people who are historically underserved by city, county, and community services."

By offering scheduled programming to these otherwise-excluded youth, organizers help them develop a unique set of skills, provide them with a place for valuable social interaction, and empower them with a sense of accomplishment about their abilities. Members are even able to earn their own set of wheels by dedicating a certain amount of their time to maintaining and fixing the bikes, and teaching the younger children to ride. The program runs the length of the school year, culminating in participants riding the STP—the 320-kilometer (200-mile) ride from Seattle to Portland that Cascade sponsors each summer.

Figure 10-3: Since opening in October 2016, the White Center Traffic Garden in south Seattle has welcomed the city's next generation of riders. (Credit: Steve Durrant)

According to Durrant, delivering a (literal) safe space for cycling is particularly important in those poorly served communities with little to no infrastructure and very few people on bikes. "The traffic playgrounds, especially in those contexts, give even the more mature and bold riders a place to practice their skills," he claims, pointing out the sad fact that drivers in those areas are less likely to be aware of cyclists. "They can learn what the rules of the road are, in a space where the hazards are much less severe." This has the added benefit of developing road users who are much more aware of their surroundings and are careful never to treat getting from A to B too casually: "It's important that they learn those skills as a cyclist, but also as a pedestrian, and—maybe even more importantly—as a motorist." As an added bonus, the traffic gardens also create a latent demand for better bicycle infrastructure, helping parents and children alike realize they would rather be separated from traffic than riding in it.

In addition to the Major Taylor Project, the traffic garden will be utilized by the Cascade Bicycle Club's various classes, summer camps, and after-school programs, as well as being part of a dedicated cycling curriculum for five nearby (elementary, middle, and high) schools. Predictably, the reaction from the local community has been incredibly supportive, but Durrant was truly taken aback by the remarkable response on social media after its opening was covered by a neighborhood weekly newspaper in October 2016. Since then, images of children joyfully negotiating the White Center Traffic Garden have spread to websites such as *Next City, Fast Company, Planetizen, Inhabitat, Streetsblog, Clean Technica, Seattle Bike Blog*, and *BikePortland*. As a result, he has been flooded with phone calls from across the country. "People seem to keep discovering it, one way or another, and so we've been getting contacted fairly regularly," he explains. "I've received phone calls from at least twenty different communities, which means there are probably three or four hundred interested in some way. These are just the 10 percent that have bothered to make contact."

But translating that interest and enthusiasm into another physical project has been a challenge, primarily because Durrant insists on sufficient funding to do it right. "I'm trying to hold the line on people having a decent construction budget, to do a really nice job of it," he says, "because I think they will cheat themselves by low-balling it." And while he had the great fortune of finding such supportive stakeholders early on in the process, Durrant believes it should be easy enough for advocates elsewhere to build such a coalition—as long as the benefits are clearly communicated. "It's such a graphically obvious thing, when you see it, if you go out there and just watch, any weekend when there's not a program going on. Some kid shows up, and they know exactly what to do," he recollects fondly. "There's just no question about it. Even if it's their very first time on a bike, they understand it."

When asked if he has any advice for community organizers interested in building their own traffic garden, Durrant is direct: "Find a great site with an avid owner who isn't going to throw up administrative and bureaucratic barriers, and partner with agencies that are engaged and interested in making it happen." The wonderful response he received, combined with the growing interest in bicycling as a mode of transport, has Durrant dreaming of taking his passion project nationwide. "I don't think that's an unreasonable dream to get a million dollars to build a hundred traffic gardens around the country," he says. "I think a little bit of seed money would go a really, really long way."

Gaining New Perspective from an Emerging Cycling City

While cities like Seattle begin the decades-long journey of rediscovering a culture amenable to cycling, residents of virtually every Dutch city now take for granted how comfortable cycling has been made. Fifty-plus years of fighting for and embracing the bicycle has made it so completely natural, so incredibly normal, that it is just something people do, without overthinking it. Cycling has become as unremarkable as walking, and it is only when the Dutch travel elsewhere that they truly appreciate how unique their people and places are.

"I remember surprisingly little of cycling as a kid, because it wasn't a 'thing.' It's just what we did," recalls Lennart Nout, an urban mobility specialist and colleague of Angela van der Kloof at Mobycon. "I don't have a lot of memories of walking. So I don't have a lot of [memories of] cycling." Nout's earliest bike-related memory is of sitting on his dad's bike's back rack, insisting on facing backwards to watch the world go by. He began riding on his own two wheels at the tender age of four, including the two-kilometer trip to elementary school in central Rotterdam.

First riding side by side with his parents, then with his older sister, and eventually graduating to biking alone by age 11, Nout kept on pedaling into adolescence, enjoying the freedom it offered him and his friends, who weren't counting down the days until they received a driver's license like most of their peers in the Western world. "Teenagers cycle the most here, so it's definitely very different," he explains. "You would be very strange if you came to school by bus, public transport, or car."

Figure 10-4: Cycling remains ubiquitous and normal among Dutch teens. No social stigma, no special gear, just autonomy and mobility. (Credit: Modacity)

It took a six-month, post-secondary exchange in Auckland, New Zealand, for Nout to gain a new perspective on where he was raised. "Then I realized that cycling really has an impact on, not just what you do in a day, but what the city looks like, where people live, and what you can get done in a day," he says. "When things start to be annoying or inconvenient, you notice something is missing." Puzzled by the way his colleagues would default to walking a kilometer or two to get where they were going, instead of using what he perceived to be a far more efficient way of getting around, he resolved to purchase a bike and begin cycling, despite a distinct lack of quality infrastructure. However, it didn't take long for him to notice the strange looks from passers-by, and for the first time he was less a person on a bike and more a particular thing, something of note in other people's day: a "cyclist," part of a niche group.

Despite completing both an undergraduate and postgraduate degree in urban planning at the University of Groningen, only in hindsight does Nout comprehend how blind his compatriots are to how bikes contribute to a better built environment. "I don't think the word *bicycle* was mentioned once in my studies," he reveals. "That was a bit of an eye opener, because back then, Dutch universities didn't really train cycling planners." This realization was particularly stark in Groningen, where he could see the lack of similarities between "The World's Cycling City" and other, more car-dependent towns nearby. "There's such a notable difference," he adds, "but nobody knows why, or how important that is."

After acquiring his master's degree in 2011, Nout decided to head back to Auckland to settle down with his partner Ruth, a native Kiwi. There, he found a niche as a cycling planner for transportation consultancy MRCagney—developing a new bike-specific unit that he pitched during his job interview—at a moment when the local and national governments were about to get very serious about cycling. "There was a lot more talk about cycling. Slowly, there were more people riding," he recollects. "That's when I realized how important it was. If you tweaked that one aspect, it could be the easiest win for changing the city."

However, Nout recalls one specific incident in the summer of 2013 that provided the perfect illustration of how far Auckland's militant bike culture still had to go. He and Ruth were out riding side by side one Sunday morning, wearing their regular clothes, no helmets, and skipping a couple of red lights along the deserted Ponsonby Road. They were spotted by one of the more zealous local cycling advocates, who was in the middle of a 60-kilometer (37-mile) ride and was sporting the obligatory carbon fiber, styrofoam, and Lycra. The next day, he called out Lennart and Ruth in a blog post on the *Cycle Action Auckland* website, claiming they were "ruining it for everyone else" and reinforcing the stereotype that cyclists are scofflaws who break the rules all the time. "That was really one of those moments where I was like,

'Well, I'm not a cyclist. I'm just riding a bike,'" Nout remembers. "It was just because we were riding like we would walk. If you're walking, you don't wait for the lights when there's nobody around. We just happened to be on bikes. For us, it was a nonevent. We didn't even think about it."

But this was at a time when Bike Auckland—the city's current, more-inclusive advocacy group—was still called Cycle Action Auckland. Comprised predominantly of white, middle-aged men who've spent their lives fighting for bicycle rights, they were quick to pass judgment on anyone who could be seen as threatening their agenda. At the time, this included Lennart and Ruth. He was understandably frustrated by their willingness to accept painted bike lanes over physical separation. "Luckily, they've transformed themselves, and since transformed the conversation in Auckland. They're now more a positive force," he states reassuringly.

Since then, a coalescence of Bike Auckland changing their name and Auckland Transport, the local transit agency, hiring Kathryn King as walking and cycling manager has led to a sea change in perspectives on cycling in Auckland. Combine that "perfect storm" with $37 million (NZD) in local funding and $100 million promised by the national government in 2014, and Auckland had the beginnings of something quite special. And while maps and drawings of a separated cycling network demonstrated sure signs of progress, nothing did quite as much to put Auckland on the cycling map as the Te Ara I Whiti ("The Lightpath"), a spectacular, magenta-colored cycleway that converted a redundant motorway off-ramp into a memorable first piece of the network, featuring 300 sensor-controlled LED light poles.

"That was the first time there was a positive story about a cycleway opening on the front page of the *New Zealand Herald*, because it was such an amazing photo," recalls Nout. "There was literally nothing you could say that was negative about this project because it was so stunning." As the crown in Auckland's fledging system, the pink path is now being used by City engineers as an anchor to connect the radial routes. People go out of their way to ride the pathway, and it's a safe place for children to learn to ride for the first time. Nout notes that it was the first uncompromising piece of infrastructure that was above and beyond what Aucklanders were expecting, and a positive step forward in a political climate in which getting out a positive story about cycling has been historically very difficult.

A combination of personal and professional reasons brought Lennart and Ruth back to the Netherlands in 2016, after Nout was offered a position working with sustainable-mobility consultants Mobycon. After a year or so renting in pricey Amsterdam, the pair decided to purchase a home in Leiden—a relatively small city of just 120,000 people, 50 kilometers (31 miles) to the southeast—but they definitely did not sacrifice quality of life for affordability. Thanks to the bike–train combination, Lennart and Ruth are perfectly mobile despite being car-free, traveling to four or five cities around the country on a typical week. Even in a smaller town like Leiden, the mobility options and quality of life afforded to them exceed those of most other places in the world. "It's the little things. On a day-to-day basis, you don't really notice it that much," says Nout. "But noise is one of the biggest things. I'd never realized how quiet it is here. The city center is car-free, which makes it so peaceful and quiet."

Places such as Leiden are fairly typical of the Dutch experience, perhaps more so than the urban centers of Rotterdam, Amsterdam, and Utrecht. "The Netherlands is quite a strange country. We have a lot of small- and medium-sized cities. I think cycling is an enabler of that," Nout speculates. "It's not the reason why, but it makes it possible." According to him, smaller cities are better for bikes—one of the reasons why the Dutch disperse themselves into smaller clusters. These clusters remain very livable, with car-free centers and retail streets, and less noise. He believes this human-scale development allows for a different type of architecture and urban form, one that's unlikely with the car as the dominant mode. "Most cities are still too large to walk everywhere. But that middle ground—in a city such as Groningen—that size of city is perfect for bicycles, and that's why they're perfect for people in general," he explains, drawing comparisons to a similar-sized city in New Zealand, where the land mass will be much bigger: "You keep people close by because they just don't travel as far, and the quality of social infrastructure will be much better."

While some of his work involves transferring Dutch-inspired policy to such varied locations as London, Ottawa, and Tirana, much of Nout's day-to-day activity is spent on projects in the Netherlands, allowing him to find parallels between the debates happening inside and outside his homeland. "We're having similar conversations on a different scale," he says. "Even though the infrastructure is good, there's still the same fight for space. The bicycles already have some space. They just need more, because they're running out."

Having experienced both a mature and an emerging cycling culture during his lifetime, Nout has a unique and valuable perspective about how they can inform one another, likening them to a pair of romantic relationships. The Dutch, in this analogy, are the old couple that has been married for 50 or 60 years: "They know about each other. They appreciate each other. They live comfortably with each other. They don't really want to discuss their issues anymore, because that might cause problems. They're not going to push the boundaries. They're not going to do anything outrageous. They're just going to live happily and continue on. And, with a few exceptions, that is cycling in a lot of Dutch cities."

On the other hand, Nout likens an emerging cycling city such as Auckland, Calgary, or Vancouver to a young, passionate pair of lovers who have fallen head over heels in love: "You can really feel the enthusiasm. They are discovering each other. They want to impress and make it a long-lasting relationship, so they put a lot of effort into it. Some have more money than others, but that doesn't matter. Sometimes they make mistakes, and that's okay. They're just getting to know each other. They still have their differences, but hopefully they'll work it out." That desire to impress one another is what leads to prestige projects such as the Peace Bridge and Lightpath, investing in something that's shiny and colorful as a present for each other. "That's a very nice environment to work in professionally," Nout adds. "But also to ride in when you're on a bicycle, because it makes it a bit more special."

According to Nout, the older, wiser, more-experienced couple has a responsibility to pass on their knowledge to that younger couple—but only to make sure that they're headed the right direction, and help them avoid the same mistakes. "They shouldn't tell them what to do," he insists. "Your grandparents don't give you direct instructions, but they teach you wise lessons just by showing you the essence of what's important in life. They lead by example." Later in life, that old couple can renew their vows, and cities such as Utrecht and Groningen are doing just that, which is an important step in realizing what they have got. To that end, the Dutch will continue to lead by example for decades to come, as the next generation of cycling cities watches intently, hoping to follow closely in their tracks.

CONCLUSION: A WORLD OF *FIETSERS*

Whether the Dutch want to celebrate it or not, the Netherlands is the poster child for what a nation built on two wheels looks like—a place built at a human scale that puts people first, and motor vehicles last. They're quick to admit they're not perfect, but through their challenges and triumphs, they discreetly provide the blueprint for other regions to use as a starting point on their own journeys towards becoming healthier, happier places. The task now is to keep sharing the lessons the Dutch have learned—what works and what doesn't—and push others out from behind their respective status quos to see what's possible once they let go of their dependence on cars.

It won't be easy. For over a century, the Dutch have been quietly—and quite happily—moving through their cities by bicycle, growing increasingly unaware of how truly unique they are as a society. This has inherently led to complacency about cycling—"What's so special about it? It's just what we do!" The average citizen has no idea that their daily lived experience is starkly different from that of their counterparts just across the border in Germany, let alone those across the Atlantic. So just how do you inspire other nations to follow suit, if you think that what you do is remarkably unremarkable?

The first step is through the telling of stories. Cities throughout the Netherlands have been experiencing their own various transformations since the 1960s. From retrofitting ancient streets to completely remodeling city centers—they've each found a way to adapt to the changing habits of their citizens in a context that works for them, but may not work for others. And this is important. Because taking a prescriptive approach to building streets for people makes it easy to miss the bigger picture. The needs of a resident in Amsterdam are very different from those of their northern counterpart in Groningen, and at least equally so from those in smaller cities like Eindhoven who are trying to make their own mark in the world. It is the ability to assess how people *want* to move that is enabling innovative solutions to their own challenges.

Just as these stories provide inspiration, peeling back the layers of history helps to identify that, while they appear to be a shining example of perfection from the outside, the Dutch and their approach to cycling are not infallible. They have made, and continue to make, many of the same mistakes as North American cities, razing neighborhoods and filling canals, all for the promise of freedom in the form of motorization. Even today, they struggle with issues such as rapid growth, lack of available space, transport poverty, and inequality. They are learning how to adjust to a changing world alongside their peers, and they are making their own mistakes.

The question now, for cities inside and outside the Netherlands, is what kind of future do they want: one that accepts the current state of affairs, content with letting the car continue to dominate, or one that acknowledges that a truly happy city is one where people come first? The Dutch seem to be opting for places where children can roam, places where individuals regardless of ethnicity or economic status have access to myriad transportation options, and, most importantly, places with social connection instead of isolation.

While technology is making it possible to stay connected with people thousands of miles away, it is also creating an opening for advances in automobiles that could be detrimental to much of the progress cities have been making to become more inclusive and welcoming. It's hard to look at a shiny new electric vehicle—or its autonomous cousin—and not marvel at how far ingenuity has taken us. Technology has been the solution to so many problems, so how could it possibly be dangerous?

Quite simply, the difficulty with allowing technology to drive development is that it lacks a key ingredient: humanity. People don't love cities because they are efficient and logical. They love them for their warts-and-all imperfections: the ruins of ancient civilizations; the crowded, chaotic streets of major metropolises; the calm serenity of old coastal towns. Similarly, engineers and planners are infatuated not with speeds and surface treatments in the Netherlands, though those things are important. What is truly impressive are the people who seem to move so effortlessly from point A to B, traveling in a beautifully chaotic ballet of bicycles, content and happy.

Across the Atlantic, these ideas have started to permeate the collective minds of bicycle advocates and enthusiasts, represented through social media feeds filled with inspirational images from the Netherlands—visual hints of what is truly possible. The cycling culture they've enjoyed for so long is no longer a secret, and people in regions large and small are demanding the same for their own streets, and they're starting to see results. Against the odds, North American cities have been transforming themselves to include more public spaces, safer cycling facilities, innovative bike-share schemes, and other, more inclusive mobility options. While they're coming to the table a lot later than the Dutch, it does not make their journey any less remarkable. Arguably, theirs will be a revolution for the ages, one where places that accepted the modernist dream in its full glory—auto-dependence and all— only later began to recognize that they must do better to restore livability to their communities.

Accepting this change—and the fact that it will take time—will be a difficult process. In an age of instant gratification, seeing and understanding what is actually achievable can dampen the enthusiasm of even the most steadfast activists. Technology is also helping to make knowledge-sharing easier than ever, connecting like-minded individuals and associations across borders and time zones. Organizations such as the Dutch Cycling Embassy and PeopleForBikes are working together to bring cultures together to learn from one another, translating what has worked for decades in the Netherlands into tangible solutions for the streets of Austin, San Francisco, and countless other cities.

Shifting people's perspectives will not be easy in places where it is still easier to hop in a car than it is to walk, bike, or take public transit even when people know it's better for them and their city. Pair this with catastrophic death and injury rates to pedestrians and cyclists caused by years of auto-centric design and policy, and it is no surprise that people aren't ditching their cars for the simplicity of the bicycle. Without investments in safer streets, matched with proportionate funding for better walkways and better bike paths, concepts like "Vision Zero" are nothing more than a nice idea.

Despite all the challenges facing the United States, Canada, Australia, New Zealand, and so many other countries around the world, change is afoot. Small pockets of advocates have been steadily growing from a silent minority, becoming increasingly vocal and demanding change. No longer do they sit on the fringe, piping up at council meetings only to be drowned out by a sea of opposition. They are now the councilors, designers, and planners, challenging their fellow citizens to see what's possible, and changing their streets for the better. Insisting that the Dutch are not guardians of some ancient and exclusive secret, they're proving that what has happened in the Netherlands is very much possible anywhere. It just takes being bold, brash, and little bit adventurous.

In the meantime, on any given street, at any given moment across the Netherlands, the Dutch keep on happily pedaling in a sea of bikes. Hopefully, as their stories are retold to them from passionate people—from near and afar—they can learn to feel genuine pride in what they've accomplished, and truly cherish it. Because it is only when everyone else can choose biking as a entirely normal way to get around that other nations will have succeeded in building their own remarkably unremarkable cycling cities. When everyone—young, old, rich, or poor, in every corner of the planet—is simply cycling, what a wonderful, bike-friendly world it will be.

ABOUT THE AUTHORS

Melissa and Chris Bruntlett are the cofounders of Modacity, a creative agency using words, photography, and film to inspire happier, healthier, simpler forms of mobility. Together, they work with a variety of organizations—including municipal governments, transportation agencies, nonprofits, and corporate clients—to address the evolving needs of cities large and small, and enable a variety of mobility options as a way to create successful and more livable regions. They have garnered an international audience by sharing the stories of residents who benefit from these changes, and celebrating how designing human-scale streets makes them work better for everyone.

(Photo Credit: Christoph Prevost)

Melissa and Chris's stories of emerging bike cultures from around the world have been featured in *Momentum Mag*, *Grist*, *Spacing*, and the *Huffington Post*, as well as many local publications in their hometown of Vancouver. Best known as @modacitylife on social media, they continually challenge the auto-centric thinking that dominates the mainstream discourse, and present a compelling vision of a future where their two children—and countless others—can grow up enjoying the freedom of unlimited movement in a human-scale city.

ACKNOWLEDGMENTS

This book, and the work that led up to it, would not have been possible without the continued and unwavering support of those who have recognized and encouraged our passion for creating better cities in which we can live, work, play, and—of course—cycle.

Thank you to Karm Sumal and Farhan Mohamed at *Daily Hive* for enabling us to share our stories with such a wide and varied audience, and for financing a significant portion of the 2016 trip to the Netherlands that provided the inspiration and impetus for this book.

Thanks to Martin Bell and Brian Patterson of Urban Systems Ltd. for providing additional monetary support that made those travels a distinct possibility, and to Reid Hemsing at Two Wheel Gear for ensuring that all four of us were well equipped for our journey.

Special thanks to the supporters who generously donated from their own pockets to give our family the trip of a lifetime: Matt Collins, Ruby Galanida, Einar Grieg, Erik Griswold, Joost Hanewinkel, David Hogg, Laura Jane, Paul Lancaric, Paul Martin, Sally McGouran, Megan Ramey, Veronica Rossos, and Dave Wodchis.

Many thanks to Heather Boyer, our editor at Island Press, for helping us realize our dream, and to our pal John Simmerman of Active Towns, for connecting and starting us on this exciting path.

Many of the themes explored in this book became clear after attending the 2017 Velo-city Conference in Arnhem-Nijmegen. That opportunity would not have arisen without the cooperation of the conference organizers: Sjors van Duren, Moniek van Daal, and Robert Smits.

Of course, it would have been impossible to complete this book without all of the people who generously took the time to sit down with us for interviews, negotiating several time zones and Skype call-ins, as well as the individuals who selflessly assisted us in connecting with those interviewees, specifically: Jehudi van de Brug, Dale Calkins, Clarence Eckerson Jr., Bettina van Hoven, Kevin Quinlan, Seth Solomonow, and Herbert Tiemens.

Finally, we could not have reached this milestone without the endless love and support of our parents: Wendy, Ed, Margaret, and Robert. You raised us to believe that we should follow our dreams, no matter how far away they have taken us; you've given us the freedom to make our own mistakes, find our own path, and see where this crazy journey takes us.

BIBLIOGRAPHY

Acosta, Rina Mae, and Michele Hutchison. *The Happiest Kids in the World: How Dutch Parents Help Their Kids by Doing Less.* New York: The Experiment (Workman), 2017.

Alta Planning + Design. "Why Few People Bike to and from Transit, and How We Can Change That" (blog post). https://blog.altaplanning.com/why-few-people-bike-to-and-from-transit-and-how-we-can-change-that-7d6da05220a8, accessed October 9, 2017.

Agudo, Shirley. *The Dutch and Their Bikes: Scenes from a Nation of Cyclists.* Netherlands: Scriptum/XPat Media, 2014.

Atlanta (Georgia) Regional Commission. "Bike–Pedestrian Plan—Walk, Bike, Thrive!" https://atlantaregional.org/plans-reports/bike-pedestrian-plan-walk-bike-thrive/, accessed October 9, 2017.

Berkers, Eric, and Ruth Oldenzeil. *Cycling Cities: The Arnhem and Nijmegen Experience.* Eindhoven, Netherlands: Foundation for the History of Technology, 2017.

Boxer Cycles. "Where It All Began." http://boxercycles.com/history-of-the-cargo-bike/, accessed October 16, 2017.

Cathcart-Keays, Athlyn. "Where Is the Most Cycle-Friendly City in the World?" *The Guardian* (online), January 5, 2016, https://www.theguardian.com/cities/2016/jan/05/where-world-most-cycle-friendly-city-amsterdam-copenhagen, accessed December 12, 2017.

City of Austin (Texas). "2014 Austin Bicycle Plan." https://austintexas.gov/page/austin-bicycle-master-plan, accessed July 27, 2017.

City of Calgary (Alberta, Canada). "Downtown Cycle Tracks." http://www.calgary.ca/Transportation/TP/Pages/Cycling/Cycling-Route-Improvements/Downtown-cycle-track-pilot-project.aspx, accessed December 4, 2017.

City of Groningen (Netherlands). "Groningen Cycling City Strategy." 2017. https://groningenfietsstad.nl/en/, accessed July 12.

City of Rotterdam (Netherlands). "The City Lounge." https://www.rotterdam
.nl/wonen-leven/binnenstad/City-Lounge-english-concept-v3-liggend.pdf,
accessed June 27, 2017.

Coates, Ben. *Why the Dutch Are Different*. Boston, MA: Nicholas Brealey Pub-
lishing, 2015.

DHL. "DHL Expands Green Urban Delivery with City Hub for Cargo Bicycles." http://www.dhl.com/en/press/releases/releases_2017/all/express/dhl
_expands_green_urban_delivery_with_city_hub_for_cargo_bicycles.html,
last modified March 1, 2017.

Dillon, Conor. "Obese? Not Us! Why the Netherlands Is Becoming the Skin-
niest EU Country." *DW* (Deutsche Welle online). http://www.dw.com
/en/obese-not-us-why-the-netherlands-is-becoming-the-skinniest-eu
-country/a-18503808, accessed December 12, 2017.

Dutch Cycling Embassy. "ThinkBike Workshop: A Co-Creative Work Session
with Dutch and Local Experts in Austin." https://dutchcycling.nl/countries
/item/city-of-austin, accessed July 27, 2017.

European BiTiBi Project. "Bike. Train. Bike. The Booklet." http://www.bitibi
.eu/dox/BiTiBi_Booklet_WEB_Feb2017.pdf, accessed August 9, 2017.

European Cyclists' Federation. "Electromobility For All: Financial Incentives
for E-Cycling." https://ecf.com/groups/report-electromobility-all-financial
-incentives-e-cycling, accessed July 11, 2017.

—————. "European Bicycle Market Analysis 2015." 2017. https://ecf.com
/new-analysis-shows-how-advocacy-can-add-5-billion-eu-market, accessed
July 11.

Excellent Cities. "Cycling Is Gaining Ground on Driving." https://www.excellent
-cities.com/en/news/cycling-is-gaining-ground-on-driving-in-the-big-cities
-too/, accessed December 12, 2017.

Fijhoff, Willem, and Marijke Spies. *Dutch Culture in a European Perspective:
1950, Prosperity and Welfare*. Basingstoke, UK: Palgrave MacMillan, 2004.

Fleming, Stephen. *Velotopia*. Rotterdam: nai010 Publishers, 2017.

Fyhri, Aslak, and Nils Fearnley. *Effects of E-Bikes on Bicycle Use and Mode Share*.
Oslo, Norway: Centre for Gender Research, 2015.

Goebel, Bryan. "A New Design For San Francisco's Grand Thoroughfare Is Finally Emerging." *Human Streets* (blog). July 31, 2017. https://humanstreets .org/a-new-design-for-san-franciscos-grand-thoroughfare-is-finally -emerging-cc12e7c0cb41, accessed November 9, 2017.

International Cargo Bike Festival. "Short History of the Cargo Bike." http:// www.cargobikefestival.com/news/short-history-of-the-cargo-bike/, accessed October 16, 2017.

Jordan, Peter. *In the City of Bikes*. New York: HarperCollins, 2013.

Kager, Roland, Luca Bertolini, and Marco te Brömmelstroet. *Characterisation of and Reflections on the Synergy of Bicycles and Public Transport*. Amsterdam: University of Amsterdam Centre for Urban Studies, 2016.

Laven, Jeroen, Sander van der Ham, Sienna Veelders, and Hans Karsenberg. *The City at Eye Level in the Netherlands*. Wageningen, Netherlands: Uitge- verij Blauwdruk, 2017.

Maus, Jonathan. "Seattle's New Traffic Garden Is the Perfect Place to Learn the Rules of the Road." *BikePortland* (blog). October 3, 2016. https:// bikeportland.org/2016/10/03/seattles-new-traffic-garden-is-the-perfect -place-to-learn-the-rules-of-the-road-192710, accessed December 11, 2017.

Milman, Oliver. "Vehicles Are Now America's Biggest CO_2 Source but EPA Is Tearing up Regulations." *The Guardian* (online). https://www.theguardian .com/environment/2018/jan/01/vehicles-climate-change-emissions-trump -administration, accessed December 12, 2017.

New York City Department of Transportation. "Measuring the Street: New Metrics for 21st-Century Streets." http://www.nyc.gov/html/dot/downloads /pdf/2012-10-measuring-the-street.pdf, accessed July 21, 2017.

Oldenzeil, Ruth, Martin Emanuel, Adri Albert de la Bruheze, and Frank Veraart. *Cycling Cities: The European Experience*. Eindhoven, Netherlands: Foundation for the History of Technology, 2016.

Pucher, John, and Ralph Buehler. "Cycling Towards a More Sustainable Trans- port Future." *Taylor & Francis Online*. http://www.tandfonline.com/doi/full /10.1080/01441647.2017.1340234, accessed December 12, 2017.

Reid, Carlton. *Bike Boom: The Unexpected Resurgence of Cycling*. Washington, DC: Island Press, 2017.

——————. "The Dutch Bike Isn't Dutch. It's English." *Roads Were Not Built for Cars* (blog). http://www.roadswerenotbuiltforcars.com/dutchbike/, accessed July 14, 2017.

Rooijendijk, Cordula. *That City Is Mine! Urban Ideal Images in Public Debates and City Plans*. Amsterdam: Amsterdam University Press, 2005.

Sadik-Khan, Janette, and Seth Solomonow. *Street Fight: Handbook for an Urban Revolution*. New York: Viking, 2016.

Sardar, Zahid. *The Dutch Bike*. Rotterdam: nai010 Publishers, 2013.

Schuetze, Christopher F. "If You Build It, the Dutch Will Pedal." *New York Times*. September 6, 2017. https://www.nytimes.com/2017/09/06/world/europe/bicycling-utrecht-dutch-love-bikes-worlds-largest-bike-parking-garages.html, accessed December 12, 2017.

Steinberg, Lior. "Making Cycling Efficient and Cool: Groningen's Smart Routes." *Lvblcity* (blog). https://www.lvblcity.com/blog/2014/9/making-cycling-efficient-and-cool-groningens-smart-routes, accessed July 12, 2017.

Teschke, Kay. "Is Cycling Safe?" *Momentum Mag* (online). https://momentum-mag.com/is-cycling-safe/, accessed December 12, 2017.

Toderian, Brent, and Chris Bruntlett. "In Praise of the Upright Bike." *Huffington Post* (online). http://www.huffingtonpost.ca/brent-toderian/upright-bike-vancouver_b_5831752.html, accessed July 14, 2017.

Tsubohara, Shinji. *The Effect and Modification of the Traffic Circulation Plan—Traffic Planning in Groningen in the 1980s*. Groningen, Netherlands: University of Groningen, 2007.

Wagenbuur, Mark. "The Busiest Cycleway in the Netherlands." *NL Cycling* (blog). https://bicycledutch.wordpress.com/2017/06/06/the-busiest-cycleway-in-the-netherlands/, accessed November 7, 2017.

——————. "Motorway Removed to Bring Back the Original Water." *NL Cycling* (blog). https://bicycledutch.wordpress.com/2016/01/05/motorway-removed-to-bring-back-original-water/, accessed November 7, 2017.

——————. "Sustainable Safety." *NL Cycling* (blog). https://bicycledutch.wordpress.com/2012/01/02/sustainable-safety/, accessed July 20, 2017.

Walker, Peter. *How Cycling Can Save the World*. New York: TarcherPerigee, 2017.

Waze (blog). "Waze Index Reveals Where in the World Are the Best and Worst Places to Be a Driver." https://blog.waze.com/2016/09/waze-index-reveals -where-in-world-are.html, accessed December 12, 2017.

Wederopbouw Rotterdam. "Post-War Reconstruction." *W* (blog). https://www .wederopbouwrotterdam.nl/en/post-war-reconstruction/, accessed June 28, 2017.

Wikipedia. "Cycling in the Netherlands." https://en.wikipedia.org/wiki /Cycling_in_the_Netherlands, accessed December 12, 2017.

——————. "German Bombing of Rotterdam." https://en.wikipedia.org/wiki /German_bombing_of_Rotterdam, accessed June 21, 2017.

——————. "List of Countries by Vehicles Per Capita." https://en.wikipedia. org/wiki/List_of_countries_by_vehicles_per_capita, accessed December 12, 2017.

WIRED Magazine. "8 Cities That Show You What the Future Will Look Like." https://www.wired.com/2015/09/design-issue-future-of-cities/, accessed November 10, 2017.

World Bank. "CO_2 Emissions from Transport." https://data.worldbank.org /indicator/EN.CO2.TRAN.ZS, accessed December 12, 2017.